All photographs, graphics, text, design, and layout have been produced by Kristin and Nigel Law.
Technical Support & Page Layout by Brian Schomburg at AlphaGraphics in Savannah, Georgia.
©Copyright 2001 Kristin and Nigel Law
www.radnomads.com

ISBN #0-9707785-0-3

By Canoe

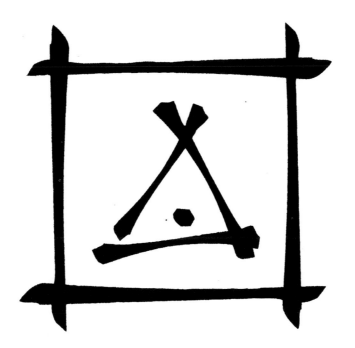

Kristin and Nigel Law

On this trip, as with many in the past, we put little faith in guide books. For an undertaking such as this one, there is no guide book...at least not until one has completed such a journey and maintained a comprehensive log. Even so, this would remain a single person's view of that time and place which can never be retraced or duplicated. Also, there are no markers to follow or check-in points, no comfort stations at the end of a hard day, no cheering crowd or brass band to say, 'You made it!'. There are no wrong ways, no signs warning 'Change Lane' or 'Stop Ahead'. There is only a path, and a will to follow that path. All you really know about it is that it is long and, for the most part, hard.

As it happened, we found our own guides along the way who pointed us in many directions, who cooked for us, who offered room and board, and who handed us a welcomed mug of beer; people who lifted our spirits and encouraged us to continue. All but a few were complete strangers whose lives we passed through quickly, sometimes in less than an hour, but whose actions helped to restore our faith in humankind. It is these people who allowed us to have a memorable and humbling experience. These are just a few of our guides and hosts, who without being asked or paid, served us well. To them, we say, "Thank you!" Leo Lichefuss...for a fantastic chicken dinner delivered to our tent in downtown Janesville. Leo's friend further down river...for the offer of his backyard for the night. Craig and Harlene, and all at the Moonlight Bay Marina...for a great Sunday session. John Smith and son...for their trailer-home after the Sunday session. Carl and wife...for the bottle of champagne hidden in our luggage. Jim and Dan, the duck hunters...for inviting us to their hide to share in a steak breakfast. Mack in New Boston...for his rafting stories, showing us around town, for the canned peaches, doughnuts, and postage stamp. The fisherman in Keokuk...for the ride to the store. The old couple in the even older truck...for the ride into Cape Girardeau. Steve and Jan in Cape Girardeau...for the very needed use of their shower. All of the 'unseen' duck hunters who laughed at us through their duck whistles...we could see you! For that matter, all of the duck hunters who resisted the temptation to shoot at the plastic decoy duck attached to the bow of our canoe. Wendy Ward and family...for a wonderful Thanksgiving. Billy Bob Fitzgerald in Tunica...for a large bag of snacks, dinner, and a hotel room on the 25th floor of Harrah's Casino. Alton and Bill of Arkansas City...for their river tales and hooch. Mack, Bob, Kemper, Bill, and Craig (the Vicksburg welcoming committee)…for their fine company and altered enthusiasm - don't worry, we won't say anything good about Vicksburg. The ladies at the LSU Library…for their help and support. John in the LSU Map Dept…for his knowledge and assistance. To all of the riverboat captains who courteously shared the river with us. Galaberos, our completely insane cab driver in New Orleans. Pete and Jamie Olsen from Madison, Wisconsin, who we camped opposite in New Orleans, and their mad friend John Parker, who helped us transport the canoe on a couple of occasions and also put us up in his old house. The fishermen who gave us two egg salad sandwiches and a six pack when we were lost in the swamp. Wally at the La France Fishing Camp…for free coffee. Patt Cucullu in Bay St. Louis…for her trunk full of maps and the ride to the library. Lee Landers at Bayou La Batre…for his captain's tales and a twelve pack. Joey and Tammy, the newlyweds with the big diesel flatbed truck who portaged us on and off of the ferry at Mobile Bay. John and Janice Connor…for their open hospitality, inviting us into their home, and letting us crash in the v-berth of their sailboat for the night. To all of the black labs who showed a keen interest in our canoe. Doug, the vietnam vet, for picking us up in the rain and giving us a ride to and from Winn-Dixie, and for being the first person in Florida that ever picked up a hitch-hiker. Hydro-Space Dive Shop in Panama City…for giving us a real chart. Pat, at the Canoe Shop in Panama City…for the ride to buy more film. The fisherman who warned us about the Bass Tournament on Lake Wimico. That dude at the bar in Apalachicola who told us how to sneak into the shrimpers' shower. Terence Hitt from Nature Coast Outfitters in Cedar Key…for his local information. The old man in the pontoon boat for the high speed, nerve-racking tow up the Crystal River. To all at Turtle Creek RV Park, especially Bob and Rosie Hatten, who spoiled us rotten for two days. The policeman at St. Pete's for the ride in the back of his cop car to the drugstore. John and Jane from N.Y., N.Y…for taking us out for a wonderful dinner. The ladies on Anna Maria Key who gave us grapefruit. Uncle Mike and Aunt Sylvia…for their fine fare and hospitality. John Jolly…for his larger than life outlook. Katie and Ron in Chokoloskee…for letting us share their campsite and cooking us breakfast. Their neighbor friend…for the yummy smoked fish. The man at Fiesta Key KOA in the Florida Keys…for pad-locking our canoe to the dock, forcing us to pay our first camp site fee, and on our final night of the trip! To Ray and Diane…for celebrating with us the end of the journey. And finally, to all of the good folks who let us fill our water bags, who sent encouraging e-mails, and generally wished us luck…

Thank you.

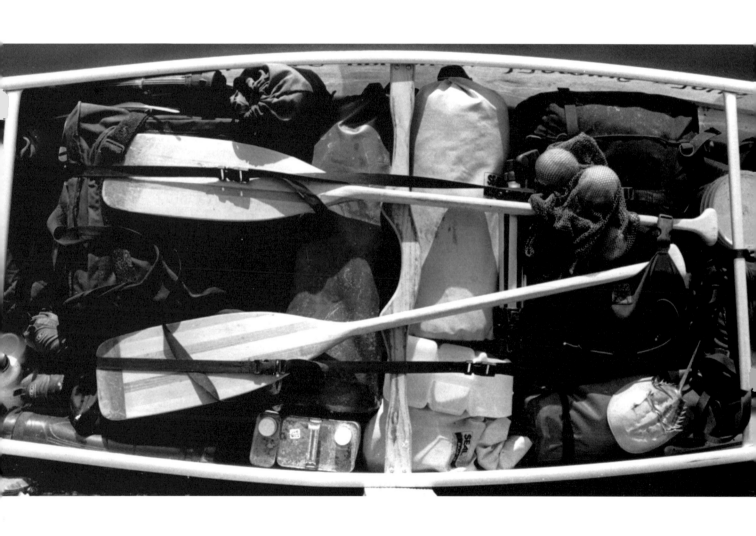

Dedicated to…

Georgia, Luc, Meredith, Dexter, Oscar, Max, Phil, Angel, Tyler, Samantha, Abbey, Emma, Mary, Max, Ben, and Isabel

…the path is long – get a good pair of boots.

Chapter I
A Simple Plan

"Every man paddle his own canoe."
- Captain Frederick Marryat

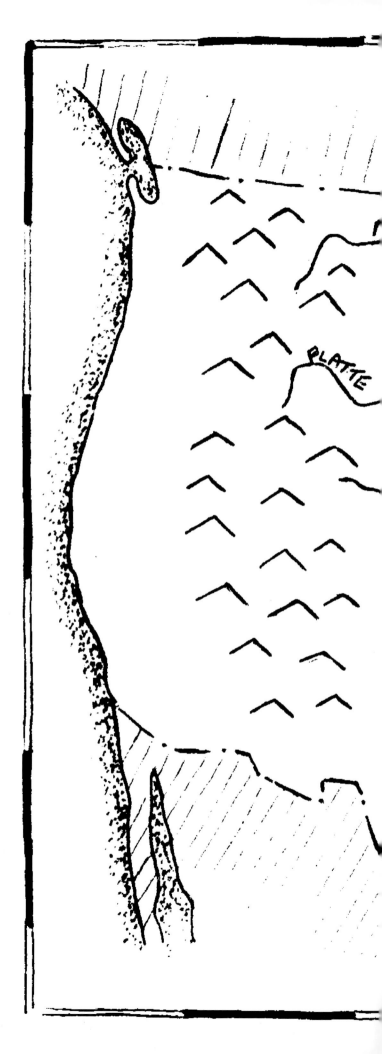

SOURI RIVER

ER

Madison

Quad Cities

OHIO RIVER

KANSAS RIVER

St. Louis

Cairo

Memphis

RED RIVER

Natchez

New Orleans

Bayou le Batre

Apalachicola

Chokoloskee

Marathon

Gulf of Mexico

Atlantico

Friday, September 9, 1999. Madison, WI.

Just another morning like any other, except that on this fine morning we come up with the idea of paddling to the Florida Keys. We are always looking for interesting ways to shake up our world and are quite used to spontaneous bouts of 'great ideas'. In order to make such a journey, we would have to leave no later than October, but we don't have a canoe and have even less money. Loosely we toss the idea around over coffee, and then dash out to our respective jobs.

"Paddle down the Mississippi" had long been on our list of 'things to do', but the reason and the means had never presented itself. Well, it so happens that for the last season Nile has been working at the largest paddlesports shop in the world. Landing a job at Rutabaga was but a drop of sheer good fortune and a most prophetic throw of the spear of Destiny - or so he likes to think.

That same morning, Nigel meets with his boss, Gordy, and puts forward the plan, along with the request for a canoe, some paddles and 2 PFD's. Why would any self-respecting businessman in his right mind give us $1500 worth of canoe stuff and watch us paddle off into oblivion? Fortunately, we have long suspected that either Gordy is not in his right mind, or that he is a lot smarter than his sense of dress would have us believe. The proposal is enthusiastically welcomed, and a leaving date is set. October 9, 1999.

And so it comes to pass.
We continue working for the rest of September, picking up extra jobs where we can...give a month's notice to the landlady, and begin packing away the spoils of living in one place for a year. Everything that can't fit in a box is sold. Kristin has two successful yard sales. Everything that can't be sold is given back to the Starvation Army. A week before we leave, we sell the bed, and a few days later the van. Cruising Fund. We're in business!

October 9, 1999. Departure Day.

Kristin sees the canoe for the first time. It's a new design from those clever chaps at Wenonah and not yet available in stores. It's made of Kevlar, with extra lay-up at the main stress areas, and is surprisingly light for it's 18 foot length and 3 foot beam. It will prove itself time and again in the next six months.

By our rough calculations the trip will be just under 3,000 miles. The first leg, from Madison to New Orleans, is 1600 miles, and our estimated time of arrival is Christmas. The second leg to the Florida Keys, approximately 1,200 miles, should be completed sometime in March. That's 20 miles a day for 150 days. Yee-ha.

In front of a small gathering of folks, we load the canoe at the dock and take the first of a million-odd strokes. From a muddy pond out the back of Rutabaga, we head onto Madison's waterways, which will eventually flow into the Gulf of Mexico and beyond. The stresses of the previous month begin to dissolve as the evolution of our simple plan takes their place. Ten minutes into the journey we make an unscheduled stop, the first of many, at a riverside pub. So far, so good.

A simple enough idea with the will to see it through...the will to will thy will.

Chapter II
River to River

"…And never before did one man's misery begin so quickly and last so long."
- Robinson Crusoe

Chapter 2

River To River

It is an amazing thing to look closely at a map of this country, to see just how many of our country's waterways are connected, and to note their general flow. It all appears so purposeful and clear, that a real plan is constantly being played out. So much of what we perceive of as our reality is land-based and dictated by society, forgetting that there are many other systems at work. The Mississippi River is a perfect example of this, with waterways spilling into it from far and wide, from lakes, prairies, and mountains...all running together to finally dump out into the Gulf, where they are swept away, circled about, and thrown right back in again.

Our long strange canoe trip began with two such waterways, the Yahara and Rock Rivers. It was simply a matter of location - we were living in Madison, Wisconsin, and needed to get to the Mississippi. But, more importantly, this facet was vital to our plan. We wanted to start from our home base, to step out the back door, climb into a boat, and then - with a bit of effort - one day find ourselves in the Florida Keys. It was part of the true beauty of nature that such a great distance could be so connected.

In retrospect, beginning the trip with these rivers had more advantages than simply acting as a connective route. Both waterways are fairly predictable with little risk, and therefore safer. The Yahara is more of a lazy stream, and the Rock a rather tame river. This enabled us to have a stress-free period for adjustment and progression. In such a long journey it is best to allow yourself this time of adjustment, to become stronger both mentally and physically. On a more practical level, it is also good to allow yourself a low-stress period to work out the kinks. We needed to consider our gear, double-checking that we had all that we would need and discarding anything unnecessary. General packing and organization needed to be refined, such as loading the boat for proper weight distribution. Daily routines needed to be established. These are basic aspects of camping and outdoor activity that make your life much easier and your experience much more enjoyable. It also can be a very difficult time for fellow travelers to sort out the logistics of traveling together. Duties need to be defined and divided, 'power' or decision-making issues have to be sorted. In our case, we had done previous extended trips together - sailing, biking, and hiking - not to mention that we are husband and wife...so fortunately, these considerations had already been dealt with. Mostly.

During the first weeks we were able to get to a real level of comfort with canoeing, learning to judge our pace and distance traveled, and improving our communication with each other. We also had to recognize our weaknesses - the most prominent being Kristin's agonizing fight to change bad paddling habits into more effective and efficient ones. Our paddling rhythm did come easily. We enjoyed the realization that our lives were going to now be filled with paddling from sunrise to sunset, day in and day out. At this stage, paddling was not as physically demanding as we had anticipated. The physical hardship came instead from the constant breaking of our rhythm for the need to portage a dam, once, twice, to three times daily. We had expected blisters on our hands, sore arms, shoulders, and backs from the actual paddling, but instead experienced strain from constantly lugging our gear to and fro.

Emotionally we felt a great sense of liberation with the prospect of living and breathing in this manner for the next 6 months. Simply living outdoors again, and breathing nothing but fresh air, made us feel healthy and alive. The water soothes and quiets. Daily existence becomes so simplified and basic... the feeling of being expelled from the contrivances of the modern world. We experienced little boredom or monotony, and our curiosity and enthusiasm remained high.

Madison, Wisconsin was our beloved starting point. It is a city of lakes which are connected by the Yahara River. The Yahara

slowly winds a course south for approximately 30 miles. We passed through a few small and typically mid-western towns, bordered by river-front homes, prairie, and farmland. At times the river opened up into lakes and groupings of reed-filled ponds. In between the towns it remains a haven for wildlife, with only critters and birds to disturb the stillness. The lower Yahara is pristine and beautiful. In places it is not much more than a babbling brook, complete with overhanging trees and stony shoals.

The Yahara then, quite unexpectedly, joins the much grander Rock River just north of Janesville. The Rock meanders it's way south and west, crossing the Illinois border, on through Rockford and Sterling, and finally spills into the Mississippi at the Quad Cities. The towns that we traversed gave the impression that they were built specifically on the river and for the river. Signs of an older wealth and economy dotted the banks. Prospering from the river is no longer possible, however, since the building of the dams. Dams blockaded the towns, with one before and

another after. Often it seemed that the towns had even turned their backs on the river. Although we had the benefit of being the sole craft able to travel the length of the river, we were continually saddened to see the water so controlled by man. The stretches in between the towns are beautiful and untouched. The banks are forested, pine bluffs rise high on either side, and a good many islands provide alternate routes. The Rock tells a story of time and erosion, always a surprising artist.

We have been asked many times why we chose to do our trip at this time of year. By leaving in early October, we had mild comfortable weather and were able to head south before the extreme colds of winter hit the Mid-west. We actually followed the autumn south, and were able to witness the brilliant changing of colors, with no bugs. October also meant that most people had put away their boats for the season. We therefore encountered very little boat traffic, and felt safer each night camping. Since our trip was nearly six months long, we were able

to travel in the South before the extreme heat of summer, and again with no problem with bugs.

After a few days of paddling, one realizes that they now have a whole new set of intrigues to occupy themselves with during the day - one of which may be nothing at all. Simply passing the time is an interesting occupation. Paddling all day becomes rhythmic and meditative, with hours of no sound save for the repetitive swoosh of our strokes in the water. For long stretches our minds were quiet, undisturbed, even blank. Breaking the peace may be a comment on the scenery, on a tree or bird of interest. Or perhaps one of us may ask for a snack or how far we've come. Few words in many hours. At other times our minds were sharp, alert, and active. Distant memories came crashing back or passioned ideas would flow for the future. When your life is so simplified, your mind becomes uncluttered, free of dust, and awakens again. Then, too, we can't fail to mention time spent playing word games, constructing verbal stories, singing and just being plain silly. There is something wonderfully childlike about a long canoe trip.

From the beautiful lower reaches of the Yahara, to the Rock and it's slow broad determination to become one with the Mississippi, we moved slowly on.

Oct. 13 - Camped on an island a few miles north of Rockford. The nights have been chilly with frost in the mornings. Thankfully the days have been sunny, with temps rising to the 70s. Three days into it, and everything is running smoothly. Quickly developed our routine of embarking by 8am and paddling til 4pm, with a 1/2 hour break for lunch.

Oct.14 - We have settled into the pace of the journey and are constantly delighted with the unfolding vistas as we round each bend...even the plastic decoy ducks and the unseen hunters in their camouflage bunkers...all are a delight to us as we pass through. Can this really be Illinois?

Oct.15 - Strong south wind all day. Camped on muddy bank, 5 miles south of Byron. Distance paddled - 13 miles. Our progress is slower than expected, with 17 miles a day on average. The dams have slowed us down considerably, and there are lots of 'em. So far we have portaged every day except one. Yet, we have no set schedule, so there's no pressure to make up lost time. One good thing about all of these dams is zero boat traffic...the river is ours. Rain is forecast for tonight.

Oct.16 - First campfire since the start of our journey one week ago. Had to stop early to dry everything out after last night's downpour. We've been beating into a south wind 20-30 for two days, and even as the Rock twists and turns, the wind funnels up the valley and hits us square on the nose. We keep telling each other that once we round the corner, it'll be better, but it isn't. The wind pushes the water past us like we are paddling upstream.

Oct.17 - A beautiful paddling Sunday, which was unfortunate because we didn't do much paddling. Stopped at Moonlight Bay Marina this morning for water, and by 5:00 we were still there and not drinking much water. The Mississippi is no more than 5 days away and we can feel the excitement, anticipation building. Camped in John Smith's trailer, 5 miles north of Stirling. Distance paddled - 5 miles.

Oct 22. ~~friday~~ 8 a.m. Behold the ~~~~ "big Mississipp'".

"Noos avent arm ~~~~" And I ~~~~ look too bad. or to w
Similar to the ~~Rock~~, in fact, ~~~~ ~~~~ see the width and
with Red. ~~~~ ~~~~'s down ~~~~ ~~~~ - that fast lane
should ~~~~ be going in ~~~~ ~~~~ much. But our pace
surf ~~~~ with the ~~~~ ~~~~ and riding the
~~~~ of monolithic ~~~~ size ~~~~ K-mart ~~~~

Our ~~~~ journey is about to take on another dynamic.
The last two days on the Rock have been tough ~~~~ due to
the ever increasing wind, and Today has been especially brutall. Last night
the wind kicked in and today it's gusting over 40 mph from
the west - on our ~~~~ ~~~~ ~~~~

Oct.22 - It's 11am and the wind is blowing gusts over 40 mph. A severe wind advisory is in effect, and the last few miles on the Rock have been tough. A couple of waves came over the bow, the map case blew over board, and one gust was so strong that we thought it was going to flip us. We are now camped 100 yards from the mouth of the Rock and the Big M. Tomorrow our journey will begin in earnest.

Chapter III
The Big M.

Kitchen Bag...
stove/fuel, pots/pans,
cutlery, mugs, tea,
coffee, condiments,
dry food for two weeks,
first aid kit, head lamps,
US road atlas, sling chairs

Portage Pack...
clothes, books/journal,
sleeping mats,
rain fly/poles, towels,
toiletries,
tent strapped on top

Dry Bags...
2 sleeping bags
(1 heavy and 1 light),
tent

"You can take a man out of the bog, but you can't take the bog out of a man."
- Bob Leslie

Oct.23 - Our first day on the Mississippi was good, but had to change our paddling style psychologically. No more bends. We are paddling long stretches, with islands to navigate. Our pace appears slower simply because we can see so far ahead and there is little change on the banks. In places it seems like we are paddling on a lake.

Oct.24 - Camped last night on a small island 10 miles south of Andalusia. There is a lot of evidence of beaver and we went to sleep listening to the 'kersplosh' of their nocturnal business. Had breakfast in a duck-hide with Jim & Dan, who were cooking up steaks at 7am. Encountered our first lock (#16), but it was busy so we portaged. Blue sky, light wind, high 60s.

Oct.25 - Got in 20 miles today before setting up on a small island near Oquawka. It was a sunny day in the high 60s, wind 10-15. Went thru Lock #17 with no problems - talked to some nice guys that work the lock...they seem to find us and our craft a bit comical. Streamlined the packing of our bags again so that we unpack and carry fewer to the campsite each night.

Oct.27- Hot and sunny. Paddled 26 miles. Heard a monstrous noise approaching from the rear today - thought it was a powerboat, but turned quickly to find a seaplane buzzing straight over our heads, scaring the crap out of us. Bet he had a good laugh out of that one.

Oct.28 - 25 miles paddled. Camped on large sand bar between islands. Passed thru Lock #19 in Keokuk which has the largest drop of over 30 feet. It's one of two that are used to generate electricity. Got a ride to the supermarket with a fisherman. More snacks!! We've started to keep the snack bag handy in the boat for easy, cold lunches so that we don't have to stop and get the kitchen stuff out during the day. Saves time and hassle.

Oct.29 - Day 20. Same place as yesterday due to high winds. Our first day off. Made and fit main part of skirt. Watched a deer walk nonchalantly from the forest through the camp. Warm & sunny day. Took our first baths in the river.

Oct. 26 – Burlington, Iowa. After an eas[y]
here at midday – very little wind and calm
at a boat ramp, just as a duck hunter is [...]

layout of the town...stores, library, post
office...etc...he informs us of the new
bridge – or rather, of the first person
to commit suicide off of it. "Well,
it wasn't the fall that killed
him so much as it was hitting
the passing barge and being
sucked into the propellers!"

ortage around Lock & Dam 18, we arrive
water. Just past the bridge we pull out
nching his boat. After telling us the

Chapter 3

The Big M

On the morning of Friday, Oct 22, we arrived at the Mississippi River. The wind had been blowing in excess of 40 mph, so we made camp on the shores of the Rock, about 100 yards from the big M. For much of the day we watched and acquainted ourselves with some of the moods of Ol' Muddy, surveying her forested banks and the flow of water between. Perhaps we had been expecting more of a noisy reception; it all seemed a bit too quiet. There was no barge traffic on this gray, blustery day, but her red and green buoys bobbed mischievously down the center and her cold crested waves lapped the shore, cautioning our high ambitions.

We had paddled 200 miles with little incident. The canoe was still in good shape, as was our gear and ourselves. Amazing. We had made it to the M. and in doing so had passed through our first right of passage. Although not much was uttered, we were both aware of conflicting feelings of excitement and intrepidation. The following day our journey would begin in earnest.

One of our major concerns with paddling the Mississippi was dealing with the barge traffic. We were wrong, however, to believe that bigger is necessarily more dangerous, and soon learned that the size of the barges is more intimidating than their actual wake. They are slow-moving, allowing for plenty of time to stay out of their projected course and to circumnavigate. In recent years wake controls have been placed on barges, so that when maintaining a reasonable distance, the wakes have time to disperse. Our main objective was to avoid the shipping channel altogether, unless it was necessary to cross over in order to get in the lee of the wind. (Camping decisions each night were often determined by wind direction for the following morning to minimize cross-overs.) It also proved easy to avoid the large barges due to the width of this part of the river and to the many possible routes through side channels.

Typically, we saw between 0 to 6 barges a day on the upper Mississippi. Moving over $50 billion worth of goods each year, they vary in size from 15-35 barges per tow, a 25 barge tow carrying the equivalent of a 375 car freight train. Tows traveling upstream are larger due to the force of current, which makes them easier to control. The size and quantity of barge traffic gradually increased as we traveled further south.

The captains and crew of these monstrosities are knowledgeable and skilled, understanding the dangers of water travel. We respect them and the seriousness which they maintain. Even the outdoorsmen and fishermen have accumulated hours on the water and give it and other craft their due respect.

Another major concern with the Mississippi, albeit an unnecessary one, was passing through the locks safely. From the Quad Cities to St. Louis, there are 10 locks and dams, spaced out at roughly 20-30 mile intervals. The water between each L&D is termed a 'pool'. These pools are long straight stretches, but they take on characteristics of large flooded lakes. There are many islands and side channels, or 'sloughs', which offer a variety of possible routes. The pools have little noticeable current, since it is controlled by the sluice gates at either end.

It was great being able to gain access through the locks and to forgo the need to portage. As we approached, from approximately 300 yards, we would call up the lockmaster on our VHF radio to inquire on the status of the lock. He would either give permission to proceed toward the lock gates, which slowly opened as we neared, or he would inform us of the length of wait while a barge passed through. It can take several hours to get a large barge through a lock. It is broken into sections which are separately pushed through, and then reassembled again on the other side before continuing on the river. If this was the case, we would often head to the other side of the river and portage over the spill dam. When a 10,000 hp tow starts maneuvering 25,000 tons in front of it, you can be sure of some major white water close behind. We soon became accustomed to their ways and they

caused us little concern.

Of course, we tried to avoid close proximity to such vessels at all times. (There was one occasion in the 'Chain of Rocks' canal, just north of St. Louis, that we were close enough to a fast moving tow that the canoe started to be pulled in and side-slip towards it. We had to paddle hard and fast to avoid being turned into a pulp-like consistency!) Folks along the way were always generous enough to share their horror stories involving barges and people, many of which we think stemmed from the over-active imaginations of landlubbers and fisherman alike.

The most unexpected facet of the upper Mississippi was that it is much less industrialized than we had imagined. Our previous experiences with the river had been crossing over it by road in cities - giving you a very bleak image of industrialization. We did pass various power plants and grain elevators, but these are few and far between. Most of the distance is pristine, and inaccessible to anyone not in a boat. Also, very little of this land is privately owned. Much of the banks and islands are under the control of the Wildlife and Fisheries Agency. There are no

homes, private buildings, and little visible agriculture. The tree line along the river often blocked our view of what may lie beyond. It's wild and beautiful - a mecca for wildlife, fishermen, and hunters alike.

The numerous islands which dot the river proved extremely useful. Not only were they interesting visually, but they offered protection from the wind and created alternate routes of shallow, slow moving water. They were also a real blessing when it came to camping since most of the islands were lined with sand banks and dunes.

Thus, our first month on the M. was an exciting one. We were able to paddle nearly every day - taking only two days off. Just north of Hannibal we met our first fellow river travelers, Bill and Ursula. They had kayaked down from Lake Itasca, the Mississippi headwaters, and were en route to Pilot Town at the mouth. Bill had an unfortunate mishap while pushing off with his paddle early in the trip and was now paddling with one half of a broken paddle, canoe style. We stayed together until late in the day, listening to each other's traveling tales. Bobbing down the middle of the Mississippi with Bill and Ursula,

oblivious to the 20,000 tons of barge that had occasion to pass by, was a most enjoyable afternoon. In their little collapsible Kleppers, they've paddled in a great many places, from Alaska to Europe. They had to complete this particular journey by mid-December. We thought that maybe Bill should buy a new paddle and get a move on - and, how lucky we were not to be on any set schedule. (Speaking of schedules, the record for paddling the entire length of the Mississippi is 23 days.) We saw Bill and Ursula a couple of times after that afternoon - once in Hannibal, and then again a few weeks later when they paddled past our camp, pushing through the white caps on a blustery day. Then we never saw them again. We hope they made it.

Although we carried two weeks worth of food, we needed to stop every three to four days for water. At times we were simply able to pull up to a park, camp, or dock. At other times we would leave the canoe and all of our worldly possessions behind and do a full jaunt into town, often hitch-hiking. We could be gone anywhere from an hour to most of the day.

We had two basic strategies for leaving the canoe. One was to hide the canoe in dense undergrowth some distance from the town. The second and more popular method was to leave the canoe to one side at the downtown boat ramp, in plain view and extremely obvious. This we did even in St. Louis when we went for a pint. Any opportunists were deterred by the canoe skirt that covered all within. There was not one instance on the entire trip that we had our belongings tampered with or anything stolen.

Taking up a lot of our shore leave was a never ending quest to find public libraries that would allow two vagabonds to put their dirty paws on their computer facilities. Rutabaga allowed others to follow the progression of our trip by featuring the story as an off-shoot of their website. We came to enjoy sharing our triumphs and grievances, and also receiving heartfelt support from people across the country. Consequently, having access to our email account once monthly and maintaining the web page became an important responsibility to us, and at times a real pain in the neck.

A lot of the towns along the riverbank above St. Louis have a quirky uniqueness to them. Attractions such as 'the world's tallest grain silo', 'the home of Popeye', and 'the most

winding street' beckon those who pass through. Not the biggest crowd-pullers, I'm sure, but every town needs it's corn palace, or so it seems. Two of the towns that were of interest to us were New Boston, Illinois, and Hannibal, Missouri. New Boston sits high on a bluff over-looking the river. The only prominent feature in town is a massive grain silo/factory which dumps grain into the barges as they dock. The town was laid out by none other than Mr. Abraham Lincoln in his early days as a surveyor. Today it remains a dim shadow of his early vision. Hannibal, as the home of Mark Twain, was a must to stop and see, yet turning a fictional setting into reality could be nothing short of the disappointment that it was. The area around Hannibal was impressive, however, and it was easy to see where Mr. Twain derived his enthusiasm and creativity.

Arriving in St. Louis was a great landmark for us, although after spending $4 a pint for draught beer it no longer seemed quite so great. It did, however, mark the end of the locks and dams, and therefore marked a noticeable increase in current. This heralded in a new concept to our river travels... floatin' with the flow. As we left St. Louis, we noticed that the shoreline passed by so quickly and how soon the hustle and bustle faded away. "Now we're really cruisin'!"

Below St. Louis, the river towns are fewer and farther between. Some towns, due to flooding, and to the Army Corps of Engineers, are no longer on the river at all. Originally, the floodwaters spread over many thousands of square miles of lowlands which created a natural flood plain, but after the flood of 1927, the Corps of Engineers started a massive plan to control the water. They built over 1600 miles of levees below Cape Girardeau. Unfortunately these levees have a corseting effect and merely cause flood waters to swell upstream. This happened most recently with catastrophic effects in the summer of 1993 when dozens of people were killed and 23 million acres north of Cairo were under serious flood. Rail tracks and bridges were washed out and the Mississippi north of St. Louis had to be closed to shipping for two months. Unfortunately, so many of man's

greatest feats are done without full concern or knowledge of the future consequences. Mother Nature wins again.

But, on we went with plenty of other considerations at hand...beyond the border of Illinois that had been so consistently loyal to our left, and through Kentucky whose acquaintance was all too brief and unmemorable. We were forever inspired by the benevolent big M. At lunch time, we'd kick back with a sandwich in one hand and a cup of iced tea-without the ice-in the other, and let the canoe find her own path, spinning round and round, forwards, backwards, sideways, forwards again...on and on, faster and farther away, in the true style of those great Mississippi river trippers who came before us.

Like a captured snake, the course of the river starts to twist and turn back on itself. There are fewer islands, but the sand bars were a plenty, for the river was the lowest it had been in 40 years. At some of the sweeping bends, the channel is reduced to no more than 80 yards wide with the inside of the bend a high, barren, sandy, desert-like plateau, scavenged at night by coyotes. The river, since leaving the confines of the last dam at St. Louis, becomes a bit more sinister and less predictable. The lower Mississippi shows it's true character, the character that Mark Twain captured so well in his tales of the river and it's dark secrets, tales that tormented the hearts of young and old alike. The river is wild and free, and has a twisted and delinquent sense of humor. It's not quite as picturesque, but it's spirit is strong and unforgiving.

On the fog soaked morning of Nov 21, we arrived in Memphis, after 44 days and with some 900 miles under our canoe.

Nov.4 - Camped on sandy river bank 20 miles from St. Louis - very near the place that Louis and Clark started their journey westward. Cleaned out boat, checked the underside - one deep scratch, but nothing serious. Passed thru lock #26 after a long straight stretch - a tough day - covered 17 miles.

Nov.5 - Arrived in St. Louis after a nightmarish experience. Paddled down the ·Chain of Rocks Canal·, which should have been called the ·Canal from Hell·. Exhausting, not to mention that a 3 foot fish tried to hitch a free ride - jumped out of the water and into the boat! Scared the hell out of us. Headed for the east bank, where we spend somewhat of an uneasy night. There's a constant throbbing of turbines and diesel engines, and the screech of steel against steel. Also there's the possibility of intruders in the night.

Nov.6 - No drunks, no hoods, no white kids on dope. By 8am, the Arch of St. Louis is a distant mirage in the smog, as we fly by moored barges at an unprecedented rate.

5.30 pm - Go for walk

Nov.11 - Camped on small island just south of Cape Girardeau. In 1838 the Trail of Tears crossed the river here. Sixteen thousand Cherokee men, women, and children died while being relocated to the west.

Nov.13 - Finally said goodbye to Illinois. It's a really long state. After five weeks, we have floated into the confluence of the Ohio and Mississippi Rivers at the tip of Cairo. Did another 10 miles further and set up camp. A very warm and starry night. Total distance - 35 miles.

Nov.14 - Another sandbar that would normally be under 3-4 feet of water. Stopped in Hickman for water. Hot and sunny day, but the wind steadily picked up to 20-25 forcing us to camp a little early. Estimated distance 30 miles. The detailed maps ran out yesterday, so now we only have a road atlas and mile markers to keep track of progress.

Nov.15 - Camped on Kentucky/Tennessee border. Hard day's paddle psychologically. The quicker you want to get somewhere, the slower you seem to be going. Can't force it...we'll get to Memphis all in good time. Estimated distance 26 miles. Clear blue sky from sunrise to sunset. Paddling has invaded our sleep and we dream of flying canoes and talking fish. Last night Andy Warhol turned up and ate our bananas.

Nov.16 - A much better day's paddling, but the river is snaking a very slow course south. Kristin was up from 1am puking her guts out. Must have gotten some bad Mississippi mud. Fortunately she was fit enough to paddle this morning...fortunate because the nearest town was 25 miles down river and we had very little water left. Not a good place to get sick. Saw 4 white pelicans today, a sure sign of our southerly progress. Camped opposite Cruthersville. Distance today 28 miles. Clear and sunny day, little wind.

Pick up sticks.

Nov.18 - A long and hard day. The big bends are giving us a tough time. Our atlas is as good as useless, undetailed, and too large-scale. Two towns that we meant to stop in for water passed by without any inclination. Sunny clear sky, but the wind was a bitch. Stopped to camp near Osceola, Arkansas. Distance paddled 33 miles. Distance to Memphis 50 miles, and to New Orleans 733 miles. Total distance paddled 850 miles. Got water from a tenant on a farm, after some serious bushwhacking. Will start carrying an extra 2 1/2 gallons of water.

Nov.20 - After the storm becomes quiet, we paddle our little contented hearts out to within ten miles of Memphis. Another sandy beach camp with the high-rises of the looming metropolis on the horizon. Excellent paddling conditions and high morale give us our best distance so far, about 40 miles. Tomorrow we'll be in Memphis, at Wendy's, enjoying the delights of good friends and comfy chairs.

43

Chapter IV
Flowin' With The Flow

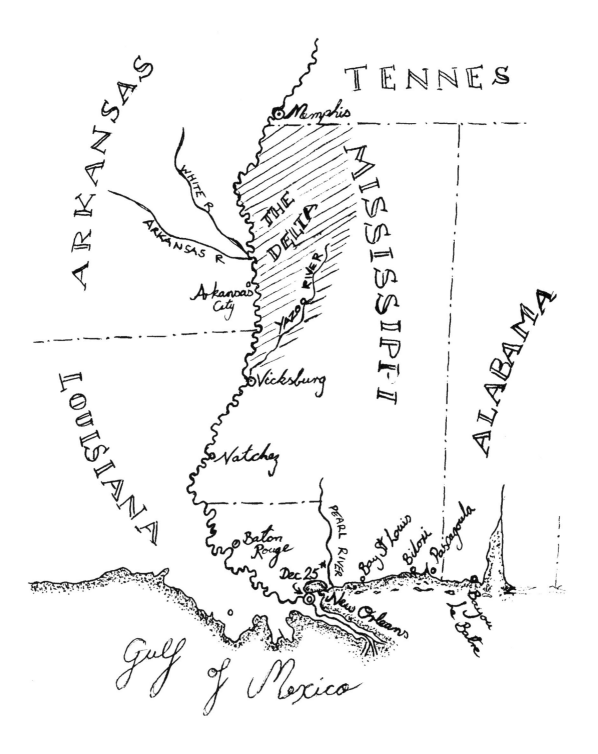

"Ya'll from Germany or somethin'?"
- girl in New Orleans convenience store

Nov.25- Our time in Memphis is drawing too a close. We have had such an extensive list of errands to run while we were here, but above and beyond that, it has been good to stir up our routine and rejuvenate for the many miles ahead. Already we can notice that our muscles have relaxed and our hands have softened, so we know that it is time to go. We cannot get too comfortable.

Nov.26- Well, we left Memphis without exactly putting our thinking caps back on. We paddled out of the urban area for 5-6 miles and then got clobbered by a huge wake. It came at us and then bounced back again off of some parked barges. It swamped the boat and soaked Kristin - not a good start. Further on we make camp on the Tennessee bank as if the last five days never happened.

Nov.27- Southerly wind right on our nose. A hard day's paddle - sore hands and mentally out of shape. Paddled all day and pulled up to the gambling mecca of Middle America, Tunica, Mississippi. Bright lights and lots of noise just off the riverbank. Very strange.

Nov.28- It was a perfect paddling day, but we only managed 25 miles due to slight hangovers. Hot and sunny, no wind, flat calm river. Camped on Arkansas bank at 3:30pm. It's so good to be out and moving again...to be back in the fresh air, and away from the Craziness.

Nov.30 - Another excellent paddling day - light north wind and clear sunny sky allows us to do 38 miles. . The radio is a good companion. We kick back for 40 minutes at lunchtime, make a sarnie, and watch the countryside slowly pass by. Doesn't get any better. Most incredible sunset thus far! Camp Arkansas side on high sandy bluff. Cold night, but no frost. Had an argument and went to bed without supper.

Dec.3 — Could only do 10 miles yesterday before the wind forced us off the river. Hiked into Arkansas City, a 4 mile walk on top of a levee, the only piece of contoured land as far as the eye can see. The rest is farmland, cotton and soy. In town it's a grocery store, gas station, and post office — everything else is on wheels. The tavern is now a flat slab of concrete, after being burnt down twice. They say it was the Baptists. We wonder who the Baptists say it was. Today the wind is howling 25, thunderstorms rolling in. We won't be going anywhere for the next few days, but have a nice park atop a bluff and overlooking the river to enjoy. Some local geezers in beaten down old Lincolns pull up, swigging on beers. "Bill and Alton, you wanna beer?" Bill returns later with a grill, burgers, and homemade wine. We sit under the fly in the pouring rain, cooking up burgers, and swapping tales.

Dec.4 — More rain and wind, 15-20 from the south. Forecast says 'severe thunderstorms becoming severe weather' for tonight. Whatever that means. We submit ourselves to another day, and also to the townsfolk that now drive up to check us out. Several geezers approach to make chit chat, and many bearing small gifts — water, a bag of pecan nuts, an invitation to the Baptist Church, a ride into town. Very nice gestures from some real friendly folk. As evening approaches, a tornado watch is issued. We prepare for the worst...80 mph winds and a tent — what can you do? We discuss our tornado strategy...run for the river and crouch down on the sloping bank. It's not much, but it's a plan.

Dec.5 — The camp is still standing and we're alive!! The wind blew, the rain came down, and lightning flashed until the first hours of dawn. The sky is thick and heavy, and it's still blowing 20, but the prospect of another day here (our 3rd) is not a pleasant one. We're too used to moving on and find it difficult to sit too long. So, we decide to leave, if only for a few miles. It's a bleak morning to paddle into. After 5 miles we have to get out of the boat and walk her along the shore, towing on until a felled tree halts our progress. Good time to make a hot lunch and go exploring in the woods.

"Y'all in the South, now!"

The beginning of the second leg of the Mississippi was spent with five comfortable and enjoyable days in Memphis as guests of Wendy and the Ward family. Comfy sofas accompanied by the tune of a family get-together were sweetly shocking to our smoke-stained nature and weather-beaten appearances. We would have liked to have seen more of the town, named after an Egyptian city on the River Nile, but a desire to stay within the confines of her cozy apartment, along with a long list of cleaning and restocking chores, got the better of us. But, all too quickly we found ourselves pulling away from the shore to the cheers and waves of a small band of well-wishers. "Bon voyage and good luck," faded across the waters behind us as we rejoined our old friend and foe, Big Muddy.

All along, we had mentally divided the Mississippi into two parts for sake of convenience. It was ironic to learn that the river truly does have two very distinct characteristic phases. Paddling the southern half of the river brought many changes to our daily experience, and to strategic planning as well.

The river itself differs drastically in that the long straight stretches are replaced with scores of long curves, with the river snaking back on itself time and again. We had become accustomed to making southerly strides each day, strides that were actually visible on the map. Even though we could see the mileage tick away, our southerly progress seemed terribly stunted. Paddling a snaking river calls for a different psychological mind frame, one with more patience, and one that we had a bit of trouble adjusting to. Often we toyed with the idea of simply portaging across the strips of land in between the S curves, but pride and convenience prevented us. Typically one S curve would be completed in the morning, and a second in the afternoon...therefore, a full day's work only to be just slightly more southward. Slowly, however, frustration and carefree nonchalance mixed just enough to the point of adjustment.

The main advantageous change in the southern half was speed. The river flow is no longer controlled by locks and dams, allowing the current to increase dramatically. The river also has an unusual characteristic in that it becomes more narrow with southerly progress. This adds to the increased flow, as well, since the water becomes more 'channeled'. At the same time, the sheer amount of water increases as more rivers join in with the Mississippi. We found that the fastest part of the river was now between the bollards in the shipping channel. We did our utmost to remain in the channel, following it on the outside around the sweeping bends. Our average distance paddled increased by 10 to 15 miles per day, significant in coverage, but not in southerly progress.

The banks of the river changed to a great extent as wide sandy dunes became the prevalent feature. This created a rather surreal and quiet desert-like landscape and was wonderful for providing campsite options at the end of the day. The wide dunes did not offer any protection from the wind, however, and firewood was often scarce. On several instances - days with high, or expected high, winds - we had to portage our gear across the dunes and to the distant treeline in order to be less exposed. Three trips with gear and a 4th with the boat were necessary. This routine was played out each day both morning and night - making it a joyous occasion when we could camp in close proximity to the river!

Towns along the river were now fewer, farther between, and a good distance off of the river. We had to plan accordingly, carrying more food and water than previously. Our road atlas proved to be misleading in that it showed towns 'on' the river, when in fact they were not even in sight on the horizon. When, indeed, we were sure of a town's whereabouts, it was not unusual to hike in several miles in order to reach it to restock our supplies. An entire morning spent just to retrieve water can be a bit discouraging. Exploring and witnessing the way of life in each new area brought a lot of enjoyment to our trip.

Also, getting our legs moving after sitting in a canoe day after day came as a welcomed change. Often we found ourselves hiking across plowed fields or bushwhacking through dense undergrowth...and not always in the right direction. Our prevailing attitude and level of exhaustion played a key role in determining whether walking five miles carrying water was either a chore or an adventure.

By this time we had become very seasoned, both with canoeing all day and with living outdoors. Less time was spent in preparing for the coming day, in anticipating or handling problems, and even in the logistics of setting up/breaking down camp, loading...etc. With time, your organization becomes routine, and you reach a level of comfort and security. Socially we were very in tune with each other, but found it odd to be in the hubbub of even small towns or in the company of others. Our lives were so different from all of those that we might come across, alienating us just enough to be secretive. Then, on other occasions, our social impulses would take off, fully wanting to swap stories with others. Of course we were looking mighty scruffy by now, with weeks of not bathing. Every inch from head to toe reeked of camp fire, along with other pleasant odors. It's no wonder we met some pretty strange people.

The state of Tennessee soon gave way to the state of Mississippi, birthplace of the blues and such legends as Muddy Waters, Big Bill Broonzey, B.B King and Elvis Presly. Typically we think of the Mississippi Delta as being at the mouth of the river down near New Orleans. Rather it is in the state of Mississippi - running south from Memphis to Vicksburg, and from the river east to the Mississippi hill country. At one time it was a large alluvial flood plain; it's rich topsoil is some of the most fertile on earth.

And so, we came to find out that there are three things that are prevalent at this latitude. One, southern hospitality is alive and thriving; two, when it rains, it pours; and three, history saturates the air as thick as it's humidity.

Upon reaching Louisiana, the weather took a turn for the worse. We had three tornado watches and a score of days grayer than a Confederate soldier's uniform. The river rose approximately a foot each day. The silver lining to all of the dark clouds was that we were forced off the river and were exposed to a more in-depth view of Southern culture, the richness of it's past, and the diversity of it's people. From the trailers and shacks of Arkansas City to the historical town of Vicksburg and the Antebellum homes of Natchez, the Cajun spice of life abounds in the ever glorious and often surprising South.

It was in one of Vicksburg's finest pubs that we were enlightened on the town's historical relevance during the Civil War. Throughout the war, it was imperative to southern towns that they retain control of the Mississippi River.

After the fall of New Orleans, in the spring of 1862, Union forces began an advance up the Mississippi...with Baton Rouge falling first, then Natchez surrendering without a fight. A week later they arrived in Vicksburg, demanding an immediate surrender. The reply was a determined 'NO!', to which they responded with fire. They were unable to capture the 'Gibraltar of the Mississippi', and were forced to retreat back to New Orleans.

On June 25th, 1862, 3200 troops and mortar schooners, which were designed to strike the elevated shore batteries, returned to Vicksburg. This was the beginning of a long and arduous strike. During the 'Siege of Vicksburg', area residents were forced to live in caves dug out of the hillsides, while facing constant bombardment from all sides. These caves remain a historical treasure today. On July 4th, 1863, following a 47 day siege, the victorious Union army finally claimed the courageous city of Vicksburg. It's amazing what you can learn down at the pub!

We had come over 1300 miles and the prospect of another 270 to New Orleans came with mixed emotions. A ratty torn atlas of the United States was truly our bible of inspiration. Each morning we'd pull it out and gaze at it over steaming coffee, and again at the end of the day to check our progress and anticipate tomorrow's.

Dec.6 - At last, the edge of the blanket of storm clouds is peeled back, and for the first time in 5 days we watch the sunrise. It shines for us all day. We paddle on, eager to hit Louisiana, just a day away. Our last state on the Mississippi River.

Dec.7 - 60th day. Welcome to Louisiana! We're excited, and also a bit saddened that the end of this great river is in sight. Bad weather has succumb to beautiful. Lush green forests line the banks. 30 miles done today.

24A

Dec.10 - Showers ahead of an approaching cold front make for a gray and gloomy paddling experience. It's raining again, with the possibility of thunderstorms. Just a case of when. We find that most of our decisions these days center around this very question. So off we paddle in the rain, soaked to the skin all morning. By midday, rumbling thunder all around forces us to make camp and batten down the hatches. It's going to be another rough night. We set up camp, eat lunch on a fire, and watch the dark heavy sky move quickly overhead. Around 4pm it starts pouring down and fork lightning splits the skyline with pink bursts of light. The storm rumbles and crackles all night. At 3am it's finally still.

5 am. - WOW. After last night it feels good just to sit in front of the fire, dry out our wet clothes, and sip our morning coffee. It was a hellacious thunderstorm. We literally had to hold onto the tent as 50 mph winds came whipping through. It steam-rolled in around 7 last night. Torrential rain and forked lightning had us cowered under the fly, a useless attempt to stay dry. We had to hang on to everything for dear life. We were minutes away from abandoning the camp and seeking refuge down by a rock dam. This morning the coffee is sweet and the campfire is filled with the joy of life as we watch the dawn slowly break. And what a beautiful morning - shocked into a severe stillness. Cloudy and overcast, but good paddling weather. We head out. 30 miles to Vicksburg, and we make camp near the downtown area by 3pm.

Dec.11 – Had a joyous and open-armed reception in Vicksburg. Come to find out that the Siege of Vicksburg is still a hot topic at the local tavern.

Dec.13 – Arrived in Natchez at 4pm, after paddling all day through shrouds of mist and drizzle. The town looms overhead on a bluff and is a welcome sight from many miles up river. It's an open-air museum with brick buildings, porch covered walkways, cobblestone streets, and wrought iron balconies. Cafes and galleries give it a strong European flavor.

Dec.15 – Cross over to Vidalia and haul all of our stinking wet clothes to the Laundromat, which fortunately is opposite the library, three blocks from the post office, and next to the grocery store – cool. This is how a town should be.

Dec.16 – Fog rises off the river like it's on fire. A cool crisp morning with little wind. We paddle 40 miles in perfect conditions and make camp on a sand dune. Today we could smell the ocean so strongly that it could have been around the next bend.

Dec.17 – Wake up to find the lower half of the canoe and the bottom end of the tent in the river. We had camped 6 feet from the shore and are amazed to see how much the river has risen during the night! Lucky not to have lost the canoe!! Cold frosty morning. We do 30 miles and make camp on a much higher sandbar!

18A

Dec. 18 – We wake to the sound of rain on the tent. Bummed to discover that we had left the radio out last night, so it's kaput. No more music. No more news. Guess we'll have to make our own. It rains all morning, and until 2pm. Decide to make a run for it, and are able to get in 15 miles before camping on an island, 35 miles from Baton Rouge. Really neat stumps of wood sticking up from the ground all over the island.

Dec. 19 – Foggy morning, thick with moisture, 100% humidity. No wind. We paddle all day, complete 35 miles, and hit the northern edge of Baton Rouge at 4pm. We had heard such horror stories about the barge traffic here. For days, even weeks, Baton Rouge has been an obstacle to get under our belt. We're amazed to see that it looks fairly quiet, so we decide to keep paddling through town and to the LSU campus on the other end. Make camp at 6pm on campus property – shhhh, don't tell everybody – Dept. of Agriculture. Total miles 42.

Dec. 20 - Rain and general unpleasantness force us to remain. Have breakfast and head off to campus in search of good things...especially more water for the final leg to New Orleans. So relieved to be passed Baton Rouge. Another 5 or so days, and Viva New Orleans!!

Dec. 22-24 - Leave Baton Rouge at 9am. On the last leg, 140 miles to New Orleans. The weather is fair with little wind, and the sun shines each day. But the days are full of the stresses of paddling through a very industrialized part of the river. Boats and ships and barges abound everywhere, all in a constant state of motion. In these three days we see more ships than we have in our whole lives. We were blessed each night to find great places to camp. After a stressful day on the water, this is a real blessing. Sit out at night with a fire and watched the lights of the ships go by - including a paddle steamer lit up like a Coney Island sideshow. Each day hoping that we have come through the worst of it.

"See you at Bootsies"

22A   22   22A

More than 3/4 of the way down the Mississippi, yet still we had the nagging feeling that the hardest part was yet to come. For most of the river's length, the Army Corps of Engineers maintains a channel of 9 foot minimum depth. At Baton Rouge that depth is increased to 40 feet, and in some places the river drops to over 300 feet deep. Ocean-going vessels, barges, and a 6-9 mph current all do strange things to a waterway that at times is only 100 yards wide. Standing waves and whirling currents put us on our best behavior, right up until we reached New Orleans later in the week. We passed through Baton Rouge with little worry, although the towering docks were quite a sight and an indication of things to come.

After nearly 1600 river miles paddled, we arrived in New Orleans at noon on Christmas Day, our 78th day on the river. The last few days on the river came and went in a strange blur. After a final portage over a levee to the roadside, we sat down, shocked and amazed in a long silence as we waited for a cab. The first leg of the adventure was over.

Our parting with the Mississippi was a sweet sorrow. The last three days paddling were an adrenaline-fueled frenzy through a big-boat battlefield. From Baton Rouge to New Orleans, the river transforms into an industrial corridor of nightmarish proportions. The last 130 miles were the source, the breeding ground of all that

we had seen in the last 2 months. Petro-chemical factories, power plants, and grain elevators littered the banks and the river was a cacophony of ocean freighters, tankers, barges, tugs, tows, pilots and ferries, all in constant motion, jostling and shuffling for the docks and moorings. It was like Dodge City at high noon and no place for a canoe. Even the driftwood was bigger than we were. There was no clear path to take. Barges on the right bank moored ten wide, towboats on the left pushing and shunting other barges into position to be filled with the contents of the transglobal freight ships anchored alongside. Tug and pilot boats zipped from one side to the other in a seemingly pointless operation. And barreling down the middle, empty tankers raced back out to sea. We went on the offensive and attacked the situation head on, paddling down one side, then into the middle, then over to the other. At times we stopped and tried to figure out where a tow was going, what it was doing. At other times, just as we passed a sleeping giant, it would roar into life and swing out towards us. Back into the middle, we'd paddle at full thrust. "Which way?" we'd shout to each other. "I don't know!" we'd shout back. We kept paddling, rolling over 3 to 4 foot wakes, ducking and weaving like a very insignificant part of a mighty machine.

After ten miles of this mayhem, an end would be in sight and the beauty of the river once

more restored. We'd breathe a big sigh... maybe that was the worst of it. Alas, five miles later, around another bend, we would be greeted with a vision more boggling than the last. And so it went on for 3 1/2 days, with each day progressively busier than the previous. It was the Mississippi's final challenge, a final reminder from a great river, lest we should forget how mighty the river can be. Thinking back to October 9th, it was hard to believe that the small pond behind Rutabaga should lead to such a place.

We were snapped out of our delirious fog by the arrival of the cab... loaded the canoe onto the roof and piled inside. Our driver, "Galaberos the Destroyer", informed us that we were in the 'adventure cab', and that we could "eat, drink, and smoke," as he proceeded to simultaneously do all three - all the while telling us about his preventative measures for the end of the 20th century the following week! Sitting there in that back seat, on our way to a State Park, we smiled to each other, both realizing that maybe the adventure had no end - that maybe it is always just beginning.

A poem by Kristin and Nigel.

There was once a young girl who lived in a canoe.
She paddled all day with nothing better to do.
With her was a fellow, who looked quite a sight,
And they paddled and paddled with all of their might.

Until one day they said, "Bollocks to this!"
And for a big motor, the two of them wished.
But they had no money, and could buy no gas,
So they ate lots of beans, and blew it out their ass.

Now, if you should see them,
You can ask if they're well.
But, please, be warned
Of the terrible smell!

Making a simple skirt for your canoe.

Having a skirt on your canoe has several advantages. It cuts wind resistance, prevents swamping from waves breaking over the beam, and minimizes rain water pooling in the bilge. We also found the skirt useful for keeping our gear unseen from prying eyes and feisty fingers. There are companies which custom-make skirts that will not only deck your whole boat but will also cinch tight around your torso, similar to a kayak skirt. We, however, could neither afford nor had time to get such a thing, so we made our own and were very pleased with it. Here you go...

What you need to make a three piece canoe skirt:
(Example is given for our 18 footer, but the pattern should be adjusted according to size.)
36ft. of 1in. Velcro
Old large nylon tent
4ft. x 19ft. piece of polythene, or some such sheet of plastic
Marker pen
Tape
Contact cement
Sewing machine

1/ Make a pattern. First, place the large sheet of plastic over the canoe. Tape it down fairly tight.

2/ Using a marker, draw a line following the bottom edge of the gunwale. Go all the way around.

3/ Mark your cockpit areas.

4/ Cut out. This is your pattern.

5/ Chop the bottom off of an old tent. (The bottom has less seams and may be a little thicker than the walls and the roof.)

6/ Transfer the pattern onto the nylon. Mark a dotted line 1 inch inside the outline. (this will be the area for velcro placement.) Then, Mark a dotted line 1 inch outside the outline. (This will demarcate your hem.) Cut out along outside dotted line.

7/ Turn in the hem and pin. Sew.

8/ Pin on the Velcro, using only the half with the soft loop surface. Sew.

9/ Stick the other half of the Velcro (with the harder hook surface) just below the gunwale with contact cement.

10/ Allow 24 hours to dry, and presto!

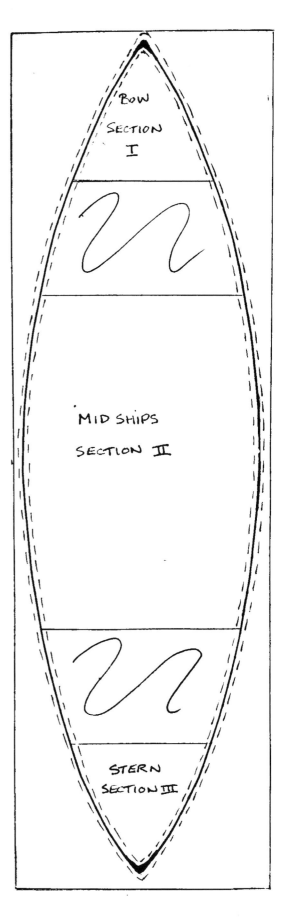

Chapter V
Into the Gulf

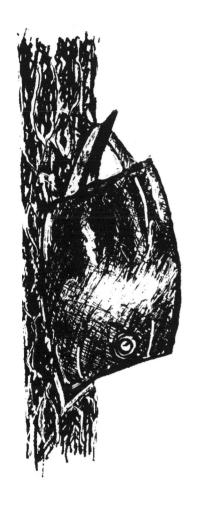

Small craft advisory is in effect...
Tonight...Partly cloudy, NE wind 20-30 kts and gusty. Diminishing to 15-20 kts late. Seas 7 ft. Rough in protected waters.
Saturday...East wind, diminishing to 15 kts. Seas subsiding to 5 ft. Choppy to rough in protected waters.
Saturday night...Wind becoming SE 10-15 kts. Seas to 2 ft. A light chop on protected waters.

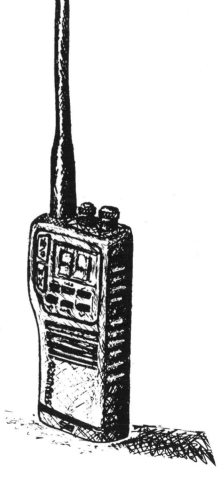

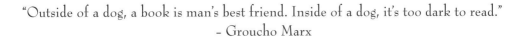

"Outside of a dog, a book is man's best friend. Inside of a dog, it's too dark to read."
- Groucho Marx

Chapter 5

Into The Gulf

Down the Pearl River, into the Mississippi Sound, out into Mobile Bay, and to the Florida border...the Gulf coast added a whole new dimension to our long strange canoe trip. After the defining borders of the Mississippi River, variety became our mode of life, with several choices offered for our travel route. The coast itself is lined with barrier islands a few miles offshore. Therefore we had the option to either run the coastline, jump across and run the islands, or later, seek refuge in the protected channel of the Inter Coastal Waterway. Our decision making was based largely on the wind direction and strength. We pushed on through marsh, open water, across bays, around islands, and into canals. As expected, the paddling was much harder and we were forced to work for every mile. We traded the swift current of Ol' Muddy for tides and cross-waves. Gone were the weeks of paddling 40 miles a day with long lazy lunch breaks, but the drastic change of scenery and the thrill of the open water kept us plugging along.

We spent 7 days in New Orleans, or to be more precise, at Bayou Signette State Park. The city was rapidly filling up with people who had decided that this was the place to see out the millennium, the second coming, the end of the world, the last chance to party like it's 1999. Ironically enough, camped opposite us were three chaps from Madison, WI. The Olsen brothers and their brother-in-law, John Parker, soon became good friends. Although restful, much of our time was spent preparing for the high seas adventures to come. A few extra pieces of gear needed to be added to our inventory, namely Wellington boots and some better waterproof boxes for the photography supplies. A big thank-you to Otterbox for promptly supplying the boxes. On the eve of the new year we all headed for the French Quarter, along with several million others. Needless to say the whole experience soon became a little overwhelming - by 8pm the madness followed a very predictable path and we decided to beat a hasty retreat.

After a week in the city of jazz, beads, and gumbo, it was time to resume our paddling. The following day we said goodbye to the new friends we had made, loaded the canoe and all into John Parker's pickup truck, skirted the edge of Lake Pontchartrain, and stepped out on the banks of the Pearl River. We could see no benefit to paddling through the mayhem of N.O. and it's waterways.

Six miles upstream from the salty water of the Gulf is where the second leg began. Slowly we meandered down the Pearl, spending two days completely surrounded by a sea of Serengeti-like grasslands that stretched as far as the eye could see. We paddled deep into the bayou, snaking between tall reed grass banks that prevented us from seeing further than 20 feet ahead. The Gulf was just beyond our vision. The bayou is an unfathomable maze of routes. On the second day, it was not long before we were completely lost. Every few minutes we would come to an intersection, and try to watch the flow of water, to judge which way to turn. The channel became so narrow that we couldn't even turn the boat around. So we went on snaking our way to who knows where, stopping often to stand on our seats, trying to catch a glimpse of the elusive sea. The sound of the ocean finally became audible, but it was still invisible across the sea of grass. Finally we rounded a bend, and BANG, 50 yards in front of us was the bright blue ocean! Kristin's heart skipped a beat and she gasped! After 86 days we had finally arrived! There were white caps and small breakers, but nothing too serious. We paused to look at it, ate a sandwich, and then plowed forward. We paddled off into the choppy conditions, attempting to weigh how the boat, and we, handled it. Trying to avoid the waves on our beam, we headed off shore at 45 degrees and then cut back in. Everything we

learned on the Mississippi, reading waves and working together, was applied. The boat sat firmly on the waves and slowly our confidence built. After a few hours we spotted a beautiful beach and decided to call it a day. Our first taste of the Gulf had been an exciting one. It felt great to be back on the seashore and we were optimistic about our ability to complete this final stage.

The first few days we paddled cautiously, adjusting to the rolling water conditions and making frequent stops. The Champlain handled the sea conditions like a champ. It inspired our confidence and we felt completely safe in fairly rough and choppy waters.

We were actually in the Mississippi Sound. The Gulf of Mexico proper is on the other side of a strip of shallows and thin barrier islands which line the coast about 8 miles out. The Mississippi Gulf Coast stretches for approximately 40 miles with little tide, but has a shallow sloping shelf which extends out to sea. Twenty seven miles of this coast is man-made 'sugar white' beach, extending from Bay St. Louis to Biloxi.

The first week on the Gulf Coast was spent scooting along approximately one mile offshore. It was a captivating time - stimulating mentally, physically, and visually. Mentally we were on a high, simply from having started the second half of the trip. Also, paddling the seas was a very different experience to paddling the Mississippi. It was a new challenge that broke any monotony that had established. In addition, we now had a coastline full of things to look at! People, houses, cars, towns, and even gaudy casinos...all slowly inching past. Restocking water and supplies was no longer a large concern, and days of unfair weather could be spent rambling around in a coastal town. The only drawback was that camping now posed a slight difficulty. Often we had to resort to waiting until dark to set up camp, and being gone again by sunup.

There were two small towns that we particularly enjoyed in this stretch. Bay St. Louis, Mississippi, and Bayou La Batre, Alabama. Bay St. Louis sits on a 2 mile wide bay. Gusty winds and white caps prevented us from crossing, so we decided to check it out. Bay St.

Louis is a quaint town, abundant in moss-covered oak trees, pines, and palms. It has some of the oldest houses on the Mississippi coast, and prides itself on having a lively local art community. A few days later, stormy weather forced us to seek refuge in Bayou La Batre. (Most famous for being the place Forrest Gump chose to begin his shrimping career.) It is a fascinating little place whose shrimp boats have been plowing through the Gulf for two centuries. Like many old towns so intimately connected with the sea, Bayou La Batre has a quiet, understated air about it. Just about everyone who lives in the town is connected to the shrimping industry, if not catching them, then making the ships to catch them. Most residents trace their heritage back to Cajun days, and this is the most Catholic region of Alabama. Subsequently, the most popular annual tradition is that of the 'Blessing of the Shrimp Fleet' each June. Shrimp trawlers are decorated and paraded around the harbor, before lining up to receive their blessing for a safe and successful year.

After three days of high wind and rain, the weather cleared and we were able to tackle our next obstacle - crossing the 5 mile mouth of Mobile Bay. We put the art of 'island hopping' to play, and never before had a dangerous crossing been so easily avoided. We headed out of B la B, three miles east and then seven miles due south into the open water, and towards a thin strip of land that was not yet visible to us on the horizon. The weather was perfect for such a crossing, and by 11:30 am we were kicked back in front of a row of stilt houses on the north shore of Dauphin Island, cracking open a beer to celebrate. We paddled on to the eastern end of the island, where there is a ferry that crosses the mouth of Mobile Bay. Oil and gas rigs litter the bay and surrounding coast. There is a constant stream of supply ships carrying food, water, and people to the rigs. We decided that the ferry would be a pleasant and stress-free way of observing the surreal landscape that lie in our path. We pulled up to the ferry dock, and Kristin went off to make inquiries. She came back with half a dozen people and a newlywed couple with

a large flat-bed truck! Everybody helped to load the canoe, contents and all, onto the bed of the truck. Soon we were ferrying across the bay! It was only a few miles, but at the time seemed like a really special treat. We were dropped off again on the other side right on the beach in front of Fort Morgan. This was the first of many forts that would seize our interest in the next few weeks.

As you run the barrier islands near Mobile Bay, the distance between the islands and the mainland gradually decreases. At some places the Inter Coastal Waterway funnels down to a channel less than a mile wide. In parts, man-made canals were constructed to interconnect the natural channels. In other words, the barrier islands form bays, and a man-made cut connects these bays. The ICW can be dangerous for small, unmotorized craft, with little room or time to maneuver if encountered with any boat traffic. In man-made sections, the canal is narrow and high-sided, meaning that waves and wakes crash against the sides and bounce back at you again.

It can turn into a bit of a choppy soup for two folks in a canoe. It is a place that we would normally try to pass through quickly. On the other hand, the canal does provide protection from the wind, and in theory, should remain calmer than the open seas. This next package of reasoning was severely put to the test, however.

Pushing on we crossed the white-capped and windswept Wolf Bay, and 5 miles from the Florida border we spy 'Pirate's Cove'. Seeking warmth and a rest, we pull up, and another afternoon goes to pot, or rather beer. Camped for a few hours that night on the shore just out of reach of irate pirates, looking for two people who accidentally left without paying their tab. To make matters worse, at the break of dawn the next morning, we slid away and out into Perdido Bay...half way across we saw the lights of the Alabama Marine Patrol racing towards us. Crap. Of course we think we are getting busted for the tab scenario. "Y'all got lifejackets?" he shouts from his speedboat. We reach under our seats and hoist them triumphantly over our heads! "Y'all have a nice day now, ya hear?", and we paddled off on smooth waters to Florida.

On January 16th we had finally arrived in the final frontier. Oh, to be back in Florida. You know exactly when you are in Florida because everybody has speedboats and drives like complete idiots. Past Fort Mc Rae and Fort Pickens, and the mouth of Pensacola Bay... we camped on Gulf Islands National Seashore and celebrated our arrival in Florida.

Jan.4 - Nothing like waking up to look out at the ocean. Back on the water by 8am. The tide is out, so we have to portage the boat and all our gear out about 100 yards. We paddle 6 miles to Bay St. Louis, and decide not to cross the 2 mile mouth of the bay due to gusty winds and white caps. So we pull up onto the beach and are off into town.

Jan.5 - The morning is cold and dreary. Again we portage out over the sand flats and paddle off across the windy cold waters. A north wind funnels down the bay and the crossing is a gnarly one. Finally we get in the lee and continue on 200 yards off shore, slowly passing a beautiful 30 mile stretch of man made beach that extends from Bay St. Louis to Biloxi. Land on a beach and call it a day, trying hard to be inconspicuous. Wait until dark and then make camp in front of a sign, "No tents, no camping, no boats, no fireworks". The beach is littered with dead fireworks, so we figure we fit right in.

Jan.7 - It's a much warmer morning and the tide is not out so far. It looks like an easy 20 yard portage, but the mud is thick and deep and every step it sucks the Wellingtons right off our feet. The weight of carrying the canoe pushes us deeper into the mud, completely immobilizing us, falling down, covered in mud, and eventually laughing hysterically. So much for our easy portage. Pascagula is the big obstacle for today. It's a large port and ship building area of which we are oblivious until we are passing by huge US Navy ships undergoing refit. We paddle at ease past battleships and oil rigs.

Jan.8 - Missi-Alabama border. A massive oil refinery a mile inland hovers on the horizon for the entire day. The wind has turned easterly and we paddle in breezy choppy conditions. The shoreline is marshy grasslands which extend into the bay before us. Once again we find ourselves snaking through pointless bayous that seem to go everywhere and nowhere - another lengthy and pointless swamp tour. Of course we have no detailed maps or charts. We stop for lunch tired and pissed off. Finally around another bend, and we are once more out in open water, but bad weather is forecast and the sunny sky slowly gives way to a blanket of cloud. The wind and waves pick up. We paddle hard into the wind, and both feel the need to get off the water. The marshy shoreline has made campsites scarce, and this time we'll need a good one to sit out the approaching front. We stop to inquire and are told of a town 5 miles down. "They got shrimp boats there", the man tells us. Exhausted and fed up, the prospect of paddling another two hours in the crappy weather is a big morale killer. But we paddle on. Across the bay we see shrimp boats and a long low warehouse. After some aggressive paddling, we arrive in Bayou La Batre, a little squat town with a thriving boat industry. We drink some beers with a couple of guys in a truck, and end a tough day on a high note.

Jan.9 - The whole day is shrouded in a wet blanket of fog and drizzle. We watch shrimp boats slowly appear out of the mist, returning to port after three weeks in the Gulf. Boats of all shapes and sizes leave the protected docks, some leaving wives and girlfriends standing silently behind. Met a very interesting man by the name of Lee Landers. He's a boat captain, a Marine Corps vet from the Korean War, and a fine looking gentleman of some 70 years. Once a shrimp boat captain, he now delivers these boats to all corners of the globe. He's off next week to Lagos, Nigeria with three made-in-Bayou La Batre shrimp boats, at a million bucks a piece. Lee shared many stories with us, but one in particular is worth remembering...It seems Lee was off in the middle of the Gulf when one of his crew spotted a small fishing boat bobbing on the heavy sea. They approached to find a decimated man who had been adrift for over 10 days after having engine trouble. The man barely survived on two cans of Coke and the fish that jumped into his boat. His first words to Lee were, "You're God!" Lee dropped him back onshore, to the extreme delight of his family and friends who had already held a funeral for him. The story made national headlines and Lee was deemed a hero. His response? "Oh hell, I didn't do anything, our paths crossed...The guy perked right up after I gave him his first beer."

Jan.10 - B la B. The storm hits at midnight. The wind really kicks in and one gust in particular leans heavily on the tent, shaking it to the point of takeoff. We hear our pots and pans moving around, but by 3am the worst of it is over. At 6am Nile looks out of the tent and can't believe it's finally happened...the canoe is gone! "They stole it during the night, during the storm". But as we look around, we see bits of our gear scattered across the field and the canoe sitting upright about 50 yards away. Unbelievable, but the canoe had blown away.

Jan.11 - Camped on beach - Fort Morgan. There's an eerie atmosphere around the fort, and it gives Nile the willies. A weird sound like a Chinese pipe floats across the dusky bay. It all feels quite strange. We make camp on the beach in front of the fort. Nile has the feeling that in the morning mist he'll wake to see an apparition of the mutilated soldiers and sailors from the many battles that have been fought here. It's a calm and still night and the pipes play their melancholy melody. The horizon is littered with the lights and gas fires of the oil rigs.

Jan.12 - Investigate the fort and small accompanying museum. Full of pictures, uniforms, and stories from it's 200 year history. In one cabinet display there's an exhibit of the bits and pieces of a captain who was killed when a cannon exploded

78

during a test firing. His head and arms were blown off. A few pieces of him were gathered up and sent home to his wife. We learn about the 20 day siege at the fort during the Civil War, and it's reissue into service during the first World War. By 10am we are paddling on smooth waters bayside under a glorious blue sky. See a group of dolphins moving slowly about 20 yards from the boat. They appear to be in couples, slapping their tails, and rolling around each other, in no hurry to go anywhere. Camp on a beach near the canal of the ICW (Inter Coastal Waterway)

Jan.13 - Just as we are ready to push off at 7am, a thick fog rolls in so we have to stay put. By 10 the visibility is just enough to walk the canoe along the shoreline.

Jan.14 - Start into a windy morning, and two hours later emerge into a white-capped and windswept Wolf Bay. About 10 or 15 miles from the Florida border. We slide the canoe up a sandy strip into reed grasses and lash it to a nearby tree. Five minutes along a dirt road we see man walking five dogs. We talk to the dogs' owner, John Conner, who offers to give us a ride to the library. A few hours later, we are approached by John's wife, Janice, who invites us to dinner and offers us accommodation on their sailboat for the night. Food, showers, laundry, and a v-berth...how could we possibly refuse?

Chapter VI
Panhandle

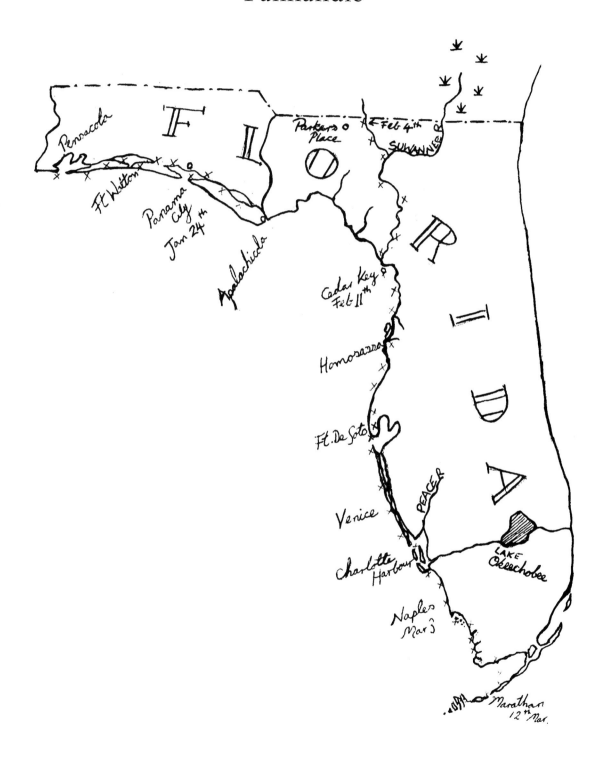

"Is Florida really necessary?"
- Pete Selbo

Chapter 6

Panhandle

Florida. 101 days after leaving Madison, Wisconsin. Our experience in the Panhandle started on an excellent note, with days that were sunny and warm. The barrier islands here form long narrow lagoons, and initially offered good protection.

We cruised past Pensacola and Navarre Beach, stopping to play in the fabulous dunes that make up these long stretches of land. There are many beautiful beaches along the Panhandle - scores of dunes that are shifting and timeless. A strong west wind allowed us to surf past Fort Walton to the pine-scattered dunes of Destin. We camped in the light of the full moon and the landscape took on a Chinese garden quality, a bit of heaven on earth.

This bliss was about to come to a screeching halt, however, as Mother Nature decided to throw us a good one. Our celebration for reaching our last state was short lived - in the Panhandle we were to experience the coldest and wettest portion of our trip. Even the ICW offered no solace. Weeks of wet freezing rain and high wind became our fiercest enemy, finally pushing us to break from the original plan.

Right off the bat the predominant saying was, "If we can only make it to Panama City". (Not that there was anything spectacular going on in Panama City, but it seemed like a hallmark point for us, simply something to aim for. Also, at Panama City, the ICW cuts inland and we hoped that this would aid our progress with increased protection from the elements.) First we were storm bound for two days in freezing rain and bitter wind. We desperately itched to move on and unfortunately this impatience got the better of us.

The next five days were spent in back-breaking and soul-breaking paddling. Five straight days of hell to do not more than 50 miles to Panama City. It was blowing so cold and strong, intermittent with freezing rain and

Officials want to alter beach access for mouse

Associated Press

PERDIDO KEY — Officials at Gulf Islands National Seashore want to shorten a road and cut parking at a popular beach to help protect an endangered mouse from extinction, but their plan is attracting opposition.

Only about 100 Perdido Key beach mice are estimated...

...ed the request...ay, the INF

on the island, said Pensacola re...dent Court Guerin, who oft... brings his family here to swim, fi... and picnic.

"I would hate to see any of... taken away," said Guerin, who... supports the petition.

Riley Hoggard, a re... agement...

thunderstorms. We would paddle all day, chronically trying to move forward. At first the wind and seas were on our beam, making it rough and tough, rocking and rolling all day. We prayed that the wind would shift around...and it did...straight from the east. It was on our nose at 25 and gusty. Half of each day was spent with the tide on the out, so we were paddling against the flow as well. Our pace was pathetically slow and laborious. Each day tapped more and more into our morale and energy level. Unsure of our daily destination, we slogged it out until our arms felt 6 feet long and we could stand it no longer. Two dry bags full of clothing - plus hats, gloves, face masks, sweaters, coats, and rain gear - were no longer dry, and did nothing to comfort us. At night we got little sleep, holding on to the tent and generally rescuing things from the fierce winds that would blow through. Each day we would listen to our VHF radio, but nothing changed... "Small craft boat advisory, severe cold advisory, freezing rain, and strong chance of thunderstorms".

It was disheartening to think back on all of the difficult weather we had come through on the Mississippi and beyond. Our vision had always been to get to the warm waters of Florida, to finally shed the many layers and paddle in comfort. Our spirits bottomed out.

Five miles from Panama City we were hit even harder. The night was blissfully quiet and still. We wondered if it was a bad omen as we sat at our campsite amongst the palms and oaks. At 3:45 am we were slammed by the sudden arrival of torrential rain and 50 mph winds. We jumped out of the tent to take down the fly and to pull the canoe up into the undergrowth of the forest. The bay was a frenzy of white foaming water. In fact everything was white as if the darkness has been blown away. The wind whipped through the palm trees tearing at their fronds. We dove back into the tent, sure that it too was about to blow off the face of the earth. The vestibule stakes pulled out and the round hatch bellowed inward as if the tent was about to turn inside out. With our hands tied, we sat it out in good humor wandering what would blow away first - our gear, the canoe, or ourselves. The violence of the initial strike lasted about 30 minutes with some incredible gusts that must have been upward of 70 mph. Finally the rain died and the wind relaxed to a more reasonable 30 mph. We fell asleep around 5 am and woke up again at 8. It was still blowing 20-25 and continued to do so all day. In the morning we repositioned the tent and gathered our stuff

further into the tropical forest. We sat out the day listening to the wind and the rattle of the tent. In the afternoon we managed to make a fire and some coffee. We seemed to have survived our 5th severe storm fully intact. No more than 5 miles from Panama City - maybe tomorrow - maybe. Another period of severe cold advisories and freezing rain followed, making our progress across the Panhandle a truly miserable experience.

A bit of a mean-spiritedness pushed us to Panama City the next day. There was so much time and mileage to make up that we decided not to stay, and continued on. (So much for our hallmark point.) After Panama City, the last ten miles of East Bay get narrower and narrower as it snakes around, finally ending at the mouth of Wettapo Creek. Past riverside dwellings, the banks are thick with pines and dead cypress stumps. The creek flows into a man-made cut, which carried us in the extreme cold and pouring rain all the way to Apalachicola, 30 miles further on. As the canal continues, the banks rise steeply and the thick pine forest becomes a single line fringing the bank - land all of which

is owned by the paper companies.

Thankfully, we met a man out fishing in a small boat, who informed us of a Bass Tournament on Lake Wimico 5 miles further down. The air was 100% moisture content. After eyeballing 50 star-spangled and glittering boat trailers, we decided we had better be off the water before the end of the tournament.

We paddled into thick cypress swamp shrouded in a blanket of fog with little place to make a desert camp. No dry ground. All swamp. About 1 mile from Lake Wimico we finally found a small pine cluster and some not too boggy ground. Our feet sank in when we walked in it. We had to unload the canoe and pull her up over large branches to get her away from the water. Soon the sound of power boats filled the air and they started zooming by. We had gotten off just in time. Some were going over 40 mph, racing through the thick fog down the Searcy Creek. We sat and watched in awe. The drivers were all wearing crash helmets! One after another, off the lake, and down the creek at full throttle. Thankfully we had no need to shout or wave at them, only laugh.

We spent three nights camped in that swamp, on what should have been a quick and easy stretch. Cold, wet, and camped in the swamp! Everything was soaking wet. The third morning came with yet more rain and fog. Eight a.m., waiting for the fog to lift...we decided to think positively and broke camp - all except the tent, which we left up to sit in, whilst finishing off yesterday's 12 pack, our Wellingtons sticking out the vestibule. We talked and laughed, it had been too crazy not to. By the last beer the rain had as good as stopped and the fog had eased a little. We saddled up and by the time we are half way across the lake, the fog had given way to a gray drab day. On the other side, the lake funnels into a brief channel before flowing into the Apalachicola River about 6 miles upstream from Apalachicola. It's a beautiful area.

In the rain we paddled up to the docks in downtown Apalachicola, eager to find a place to dry out. Later, with a bit of local information under our belts, we continued up the bayou to the shrimp boat docks, and camped behind a stack of lobster pots. We showered in the fishermen's restrooms and went to bed clean and happy that this leg had come to an end. It was Super Bowl Sunday.

By the time we had reached Apalachicola, we decided to turn our two part journey into three. The seagrass trail on the Big Bend will have to wait for another time. The lack of high and dry ground, our tired performance, and the cold and wet wintry conditions pushed us to alter our route. We reserve the right to change our minds as and when we please - that's one of the beauties of life. As MacArthur once said, "We are not retreating, only advancing in another direction".

The next day we walked a half mile back downtown and by midday had made contact with John Parker, canoe sherpa extraordinaire; by evening fall we were driving at a good rate of knots along the coastal highway, on our way to his big old house in Madison, on the Georgia/Florida border.

Jan.17 - Breakfast at Pensacola Beach on the boardwalk. The day is sunny and warm. Perfect for getting some miles under our belt. Camp near Navarre Beach and play in the beautiful massive sand dunes until sundown.

Jan.19 - A strong north wind kicks in and by 10am we have paddled our last stroke. Landed on a lush Piney Point that is covered with pines and palmetto palms that were once so bountiful along this coast. Unfortunately the land is prime real estate that is about to be developed into homes for the uncreative. We went for a walk through the woods and came upon little signs every 20 yards which were stuck in the dirt and read, "Future home of Mr. & Mrs. So-and-so." Pretty sad.

Apalachicola

Jan.21 - By 6 pm we're exhausted but have managed to paddle 20 miles, which is quite amazing for the conditions. The boat was rocking and rolling all day, but once again it performs excellently. We camp under a magnolia tree pleased with the day's hard and strenuous work. Looking forward to being back in the protection of the canal. Will this bitter cold wind ever die down?

Jan.23 - The morning brings rain and a forecast of thunderstorms, again. We paddle the 4 miles to Westbay, a bridge and a few houses, in the pouring rain. We have no water and few groceries. After talking to the woman at the bait shop, we decide to try and hitch a ride to the Winn-Dixie on Panama Beach, 5 miles south. We are soaked to the skin and the road is one less traveled. Finally a car pulls over. It's Doug, a Vietnam vet on his way to the laundromat. Hallelujah! We do our shopping and haul a half a dozen grocery bags to the side of the highway. We look pretty trashy trying to thumb a ride with our week's shopping. We start walking. Ten minutes later Doug pulls over and we jump in excitedly. By 1pm we're back on the water paddling under a dark and stormy sky. At another Piney Point we make camp. The wind is calm but the sky looks ominous and threatening.

Jan.24- Storm bound again! We've been crouched in the tent all day - reading, writing, talking...listening to the wind and the rain. The only real chore is to keep the fire burning, and to make the occasional cup o' joe.... We've been over the maps so many times we can't even bother to look at them again. Every few hours we tune in to the VHF radio. Rain, rain, and more rain. We're still managing to smile, tho, so we're not doing too bad.

Jan.26- Had to spend the morning at the ol' library which is right on the water (Panama City). Emails are coming in from all over the country; people following the trip on the website and cheering us on. We really needed to hear that today and appreciate it so. By 2pm we are out on the water heading SE across East Bay. A NE wind pushes us along as we surf forward on 1 foot waves. We make good time and camp in the trees, 14 miles closer to the Keys.

Super bowl Sunday.

Jan.28 - 10 miles up the canal. We woke to the sound of light rain on the tent. Apart from the extreme cold, there's a 70% chance of rain and thunderstorms this afternoon. The canal is smooth and the thought of paddling another 20 miles is tempting. But we decide we better stay put. Paddling in the rain in this temperature would be no fun and probably dangerous. We can't be guaranteed of a campsite when we might need it. By 9:30am it's really raining and we are tent bound, eating and reading the day away. Rain is forecast for the next 3-4 days, along with very cold night time temperatures. We try to keep busy and keep our spirits up. If we can just make it to Apalachicola...

Chapter VII
In and Back Out

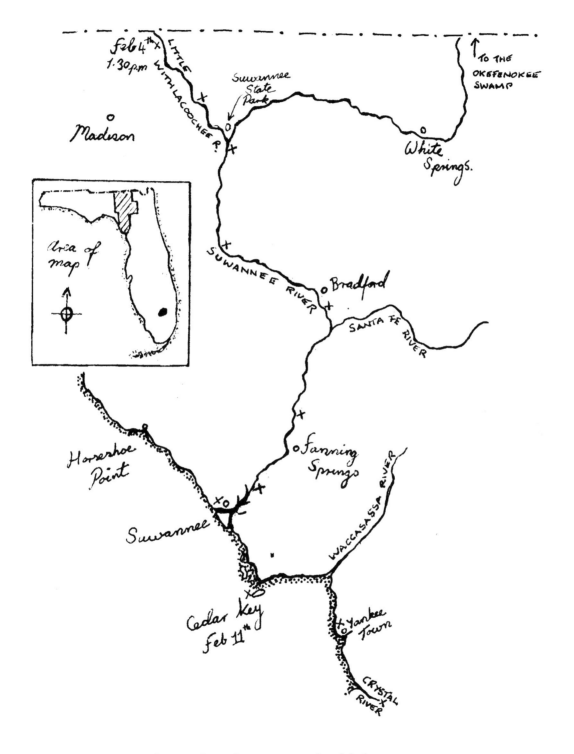

"A girl must always leave room in her life for spontaneity."
- Currie Butzbaugh

In and Back Out

Rerouting took us northeast and inland to the Georgia/Florida border to hook up with the Little Withlacoochee and Suwannee Rivers. But first, we enjoyed a sabbatical with our new and delightfully mad friend, John Parker. John is a Wisconsin native who has transplanted himself to northern Florida and purchased a formidable undertaking in the form of a dilapidated old farmhouse from the 1830s. It remains one of the oldest structures of it's kind, and the task of renovating it would have put fear in any reasonable person's soul. But, fortunately, John is a not a reasonable person. He acquired a tangled pile of pine planks and will no doubt one day be the proud owner of a war/history museum. He bears witness to what two hands can accomplish against great odds, and for perhaps this reason, we found ourselves an ally. After two days R&R, the right honorable Mr. Parker drove his canoe cab to the banks of the Withlacoochee and we soon found ourselves paddling away between low rocky cliffs down it's dark waters. (Further from the Keys than we were a week before.)

River relief came sweetly as we bounced off every rock in the little rapids of this beautiful ancient waterway. We were constantly negotiating small rapids and had to do quite a difficult portage, first scaling up a steep rocky bank and then bushwhacking through dense undergrowth. Rounded boulders protrude out of the water and the banks are pitted limestone. We camped that first night on a gorgeous bend in the river. It felt like it had been a campsite for as long as people have walked this part of the earth. Indeed, the Withlacoochee River seems as old as the hills and is still untouched along most of it's course.

Late the following day, we flowed into the black waters of the famous Suwannee River, the sixth river of our journey so far.

The Suwannee river bank is dotted with houses, docks, and piers in varying states of

From the little Withlacoochee

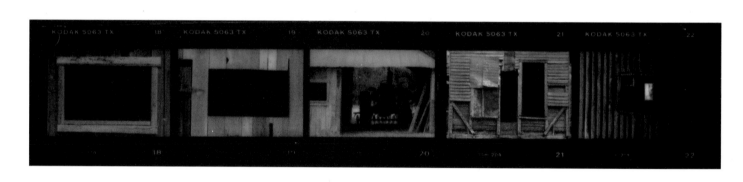

... and onto Ol' Suwannee

Feb. 2-3 - John Parker's old house will rise again and to a greater glory. For shade and beauty it has some of the oldest and largest trees in the state. We were entertained with fine vitals and song. Our brief stay included a 100 foot ring of fire burning in his yard and an awesome rendition of the Star Spangled Banner on his electric guitar! We also reenacted a Civil War battle with some 500 hand-painted miniature figures. At one point we thought that Johnny Reb was going to win, but them fancy Yankees had him out-gunned and out-smarted. The evenings have been very chilly, but gloriously starry. Tomorrow we will resume our journey south and hopefully to warmer climes.

Feb. 8 - Just before 8am we are off on a very twisty section of the river. Some cloud cover which is nice because the sun is intense reflecting off of the black water of the Suwannee. Apart from a couple of fishermen, we see no one - it's so very quiet. We make excellent time, more than 20 miles, but have some difficulty finding a campsite. Most of the land is private property.

Feb. 9 - The swamp. Another hot sunny day. The river flows along at a lazy pace and it feels great to be sitting atop of it. We pass fewer dwellings and the river takes more of a natural and swampy appearance. With only one hour before dark, we had no choice but to camp on low swampy ground somewhere between Manatee Springs and Fowler Bluff. The bank is a mass of woven root systems and critter caverns that recede back and hold up the forest floor; hopefully not home to sleeping gators. Paranoia kicks in just as the last lick of light has well and truly left the forest, and Kristin informs me that only yesterday her mom dreamt that we were munched by gators. Around midnight we are woken by heavy rustling. I grab the headlamp, slowly creep out of the tent, and shine the light into the root caves. I can hear it moving. I look around for a stick, but it's a swamp and sticks fall apart in your hands. Suddenly the glistening of scales moves through the light. The hard-skinned creature moves quickly beneath the bank. "Jesus Christ! We've camped next to a bloody gator cave!" I shine the light into the cave again, and soon a long snout on a goofy face appears. It's a huge armadillo! Big sigh of relief. He trots off into the swamp making a frightful racket and comes back around the same way at about 4:30 am. It's a fairly sleepless night. The screen door on the tent is also not working - a most timely breakdown.

Feb. 10 - Glad to see the sun come up as we make coffee to the screams of a mouse in the clutches of a hawk flying low across the river. Today we will arrive in Suwannee and once again be back on the Gulf - navigating shallows and razor sharp oyster beds. By midday, Suwannee comes into view.

disrepair. Apart from a couple of fisherman, we saw no one - so very quiet. We made excellent time, more than 20 miles a day, but had some difficulty finding a campsite. Most of the land is private property. As we progressed, the rocky banks gave way to cypress stumps and small trees. Initially, the banks were steep at 15-20 feet high. They then become no more than 8 feet high, sloping back much more gradually.

The rivers on the west coast of Florida are created by a massive underground system of springs and caves that make up the Florida Aquifer. These springs flow up at enormous rates, creating crystal clear waters that lead down into the Gulf. They are visible as you travel down the river, often as side pockets or pools of water. The clear water beckons the weary traveler to pull over and drink, or simply admire. They are a mecca for spelunking divers who explore this system of underground waterways. There are also many rope swings along the river - swings and trapezes of all configurations! It's a small wonder we got any paddling done!

Although the mornings were frosty and cold, by mid-day the sun would heat things up to the pleasant 60s. With a slight north wind and zero boat traffic, we made good time and our spirits were high. It turned out to be the perfect respite from our previous fatigue in the Panhandle. The sun shimmered on the black water and reflected off of every leaf. In just a few days we saw enough wildlife to perk our interest once again. Packs of buzzards crowded the dead tree tops. Osprey and eagle challenged each other in aerial combat, and all the while in the tannic depths, alligators snoozed. We also had a bit of a frightful encounter one evening with a giant and overzealous armadillo!

A few words on our friend the alligator...The American alligator (Alligator Mississippiensis) is found in nine states - Texas, Louisiana, Mississippi, Arkansas, Alabama, Georgia, North Carolina, South Carolina, and Florida. Our journey took us through six of these states, with Louisiana and Florida having the highest populations. From Arkansas onward, we heard plenty of warnings and gruesome tales

from folks along the way... such as the boy who went fishing with his little brother, only to return home empty handed and alone. A gator can lunge over half it's body length out of the water. Upon trapping it's prey between it's jaws, will then either swallow it whole or will drag it to the bottom of the river, snagging it on a sunken log and marinating it for a later snack. It wasn't until we were in the swamps of northern Florida that the thought of gator wrestling began to cause a few sleepless nights. Some reports put the gator population in Florida at 3 million, in a state that claims 3.1 million acres in inland fresh waterways. Rivers, lakes, canals, ponds, potholes and swamps, not to forget city parks and golf courses, all make up the creature's habitat. It's numbers today are a relief, since in 1973 it had been added to the endangered species list. Habitat loss remains a serious threat to this remarkable animal which is now 180 million years old.

In most areas alligators remain dormant from approximately October to March, as colder temperatures dictate their annual sleep. They are cold-blooded and need heat to be active. As the temperature drops, their heartbeat slows and respiration almost ceases. This bit of good timing, along with our evening temperatures dropping into the 20s, allowed us to go without a gator encounter. It didn't, however, allow us to relax our senses.

A mile or so from the Gulf lies the town of Suwannee. Suwannee consists of a clump of small stilt structures and wooden boat houses nestled on the banks of the river. The town itself doesn't amount to much - a post office, restaurant, and general store - but it was slightly more impressive to us since all are accessible by canal.

Pulling out at sun-up the next day, the residents of the RV park where we had camped were oblivious to both our arrival and departure. We back paddled away from town to the east pass. A few fisherman passed, but the town was silent and bathed in golden sunlight. Out into the shallows of Suwannee Sound...the Sound itself is made by a long reef some 2-3 miles off

shore. Stopping on Deer Island for our morning coffee, we thought at first that we had landed on a private island with it's own air strip, but then realized that the horrendously loud and obtrusive noise shattering the morning calm was an airboat. Airboats were invented in Florida at the turn of the century, specifically for traveling across the low marshlands and grassy savannahs of the Everglades. Although they do work extremely well for their purpose, the reality is that they are extremely noisy and allow people to invade areas where they have no business being. Since the main purpose of air boat tours is to view wildlife, we wonder just how this can be achieved in a craft with a noise level louder than an afternoon at the Indianapolis 500. Air boat tours - give us a break.

We pushed through a southerly wind, reached Cedar Key, and pulled up to the town cemetery. The town is surrounded by the ocean and down every street you can see water. It has a lot of character and is one of the last remaining towns of the Old Florida style.

The coastal landscape of the west coast of Florida consists of seagrass and swampland, rather than beach. The water is also shallow for miles off shore. This translates into tricky conditions no matter what the weather. It was a never ending search for a piece of high ground for either a campsite or simply a place to rest. Also, the affects of the tides are more extreme and difficult to portage across. In the morning the waterline had receded to the horizon, meaning several trips with our gear and the boat through muddy flats and sharp oyster beds. Nevertheless, we made good time, spurred on by the thought of only another 400 miles to go.

At Homosassa Springs we were the honored guests of Bob and Rosie Hatten. We met the Hattens via email after they read about our adventure in a Mississippi Gulf Coast newspaper. Not long ago Bob and Rosie cast off the shackles of living in one place, hooked up the trailer to their truck, and now label themselves full-time R.V.ers. "Home is where we park it!", and at this particular time it was at the Turtle Creek Campground on the Homosassa River.

For two days they spoiled us rotten as another storm rolled by. Once again we paddled away from a dock full of well-wishers. Our spirits were as high as they had ever been.

The Homosassa River opens up into the Chassohowitska Wildlife Refuge, which is the last piece of extensive wilderness until the Ten Thousand Islands just north of the Everglades. In between is nearly 200 miles of prime real estate development, with no riffraff allowed.

Feb.12 — A gray windy day. Waccasassa Bay is shallow and full of oyster shoals. The wind is 10-15 mph from the south. The entire coast is seagrass and inhospitable. It's a hard day's paddle. We are unable to stop paddling because we get blown inshore and into the shoals. There are few obvious campsites, and we decide to push on as far as we can. We find a small island hammock that makes a sweet spot for the night. After a tough and troublesome day, we decide to name it — Island of Tranquillity. It's for sale. The night is clear and still.

Feb.13 — We decide to try and make Crystal River before the wind kicks in this afternoon. The obstacle for today is a walled channel that sticks 5 miles out into the ocean from a huge power station. There is a cut, but it's right at the end. It's at this cut that we meet Ted — a crazy traveling dude, traveling via his "perfect solution"... an inflatable catamaran. Except it's not perfect because it's too heavy — looks pretty funky as well. He's also heading for the Keys, from Oklahoma. The water is flat calm as is the wind. We paddle into the very busy Crystal River. It's a manatee zone, but it doesn't stop the power boaters from doing 30 mph. After a few miles a nice old gentleman offers us a tow and we say, "Sure!" With the boat stopped alongside his pontoon boat, we cruise into Crystal Springs.

Ted with his 'perfect solution'

Hammocks!

Feb. 16 – Through the reed grasses that are now so familiar to us, and into the shallows of the Chassahowitzka Wildlife Refuge (a navigational nightmare on the scale of the 10,000 islands!). We succumb to paddling out and around rather than looking for shortcuts that invariably take forever. Not until midday are we heading due south, about 4 miles from the shoreline. The wind is calm and the Gulf is as smooth as glass. The best day yet since hitting the Gulf. We paddle in these conditions all day until we reach beach at Pine Island, a beach full of half naked people. It's no good for camping, but K sees a small island hammock 2 miles away. We check it out. A little palm island with a good landing beach and small fire pit on the east side. The moon is bright and the wind calm. We are pleased with our progress about 20 miles and our beautiful little home for the night.

Feb. 17 – The tide is far out. Oyster beds are everywhere. After dragging the canoe to the waterline and loading up, we walk out for an hour into deeper water. Once again, the sea is like glass as we start paddling about a mile or so off shore. We paddle all day in water no more than 2 foot deep. It's hotter than yesterday, and once again we make good progress. At 3:30pm we land on Durney Key, not on our map, and about 1/4 mile off Port Richey. In the distance we can see the tall chimney in Tarpon Springs, and on the horizon Anclote Key. Tomorrow we shall reach the point where our previous sailing trip ended. Back in familiar territory.

Chapter VIII
There Goes the Neighborhood

Q – "Where do you go to the bathroom?"
A – "Anywhere we want to."

There Goes the Neighborhood

Civilization comes hard and fast in south Florida. From Little Caladesi Key, just north of Tampa, and down to the Everglades, it's a pleasure boater's paradise, a mecca for capitalist crackheads, and an environmental disaster zone. Unfortunately, southern Florida has long had the knack for justifying any money making scheme - regardless of cost, engineering difficulty, or morality. Therefore, the only species which is not under threat is the consumers that flock there. The only portion of the United States mainland to have a subtropical climate with diverse flora and fauna has been hacked, drained, plowed, and covered in concrete. Whether you run oceanside or in the ICW, the predominant feature of the landscape is that of past or current construction. The thought that man has even mustered the trouble to conquer the swamps and the mangroves is mind boggling. The main coastal vegetation in southern Florida is the mangrove tree, a strong and hearty tree able to thrive in salt water. They interweave themselves into thick, mangled, and impassable forests with root systems running to the waterline.

When De Soto and his force of 600 landed here in 1539, they were confronted with extremely dense forest and swampland. Unfortunately this was the beginning of it's demise into an unnatural and unrecognizable environment. Had it not been for the likes of Marjorie Stonehouse Douglas and a few other cronies, the Everglades National Park would now undoubtedly be a subdivision between Naples and Miami.

For just over two weeks, we paddled down the 'condo coast'. Diligently we practiced the art of subterfuge camping, setting up camp after dark and leaving the beach by sunup. We had to avoid the ICW on the weekends, when it becomes a navigational nightmare, with huge cigarette boats racing up and down the channel at 40 mph... a cacophony of pleasure craft completely oblivious to any but the most basic 'rules of the road'. 'Red, right, returning' seemed to be the extent of their boating knowledge.

The only thing worse than Saturday around Tampa on the ICW is Sunday. One fine weekend we had the pleasure of battling the power boaters' and their wakes for two glorious days. This does not stand as a very good example of one of our better planning strategies! They navigate their boats with complete abandonment for water safety and courteousness. Even the big motor yachts, who you would think have better knowledge, seem completely oblivious to our little craft. Huge power boats raced past us no more than 20 feet away. The champlain rode the conditions well, but our worry came from being run down due to their recklessness. There were so many boats going up and down, it was more like an interstate highway. By Sunday afternoon we had had enough and landed on a small island opposite John's Pass. Unfortunately the island was also full of idiots who proceeded to leave all their garbage behind. At sundown the island was deserted, except of course for us and a couple of crackheads. The only thing to do was to give each other hair cuts and hope for the best.

By 9pm that night, the island was invaded by more crack-smoking pirates, and their children! They built a fire big enough to alert the British Navy, all the while shouting and yelling. They raced to and from the island on their little speed boat all night long. With no sleep, we slipped from the island around 4am and paddled through St. Petersburg under the light of the silvery moon. The dark canals were fringed with the light of the sleeping city and the wind was calm. It was an unforgettable quiet.

Mullet Key was next on our itinerary. It is home to De Soto State Park, a fort and wide sweeping beach. Mullet Key was to be our departure point for crossing Tampa Bay - it turned out to be a very enjoyable holding ground as we waited for three days for the weather to change. Just as we arrived on Mullet, the wind kicked in and Tampa Bay became full of chop and white caps. We decided we had better wait it out, found a secluded beach and made camp,

covering the tent with branches and hiding the boat in the bush, hoping to avoid any encounters.

The north wind blew hard all night and continued to do so for three days. We perched on the edge of Tampa Bay, looking for a window of opportunity to make our crossing. On the third day we sat nervously looking out across the bay, eager to go. We watched for quite some time, trying to read the wind and the water. The bay was full of white caps. Just as we made ready to cross, we spotted an oncoming tanker...a very timely occurrence, for ten minutes later the wind doubled in strength and the bay became more than unfriendly. An hour went by before the bay settled back down. It was now or later, so we went for it, wearing our life jackets for the first time on the trip. Half way across the bay the white caps had all but gone, and only a rocking swell hindered our progress. We crossed in one hour and fifteen minutes, and landed on Anna Maria's north shore. Ten minutes later Kristin went off with some elderly women for some grapefruits, and Nile got to talking with John and Jane from New York. They invited us to dinner at a small restaurant at the end of a pier. It was a great way to celebrate our crossing and to share our excitement with some good people.

By 8am the next morning, we were finally on our way southward, passing Long Boat Key, and making a straight path for our wildly eccentric relatives, Aunt Sylvia and Uncle Mike - who by the way have got to be the two most interesting people residing in Nokomis, Florida. They showered us with good food, hospitality, and their own unique brand of disgruntled humor. It was in fact just what we needed at this time, and was our last evening of modern comfort for the remainder of the trip.

Following the metro areas of Nokomis and Venice, the Condo Coast is briefly broken by the beauty of Charlotte Harbor and it's barrier islands of Sanibel, Captiva, North Captiva, and Cayo Costa. North Captiva stood out as being particularly wild and beautiful. Tucked behind the islands are perfect little hideaways for anchoring up - sailboats, power boats, kayaks, and canoes can gather amongst the clumps of mangroves to both gain protection from the elements and to enjoy the solitude. We spent three days here, bearing witness to dolphins, ibis, osprey, pelicans, and raccoons, all going about their funny business.

During this chapter of the trip, we met and spoke to more people than in any other. Just north of Naples we met our last fellow adventurer, a young man by the name of Jolly, John Jolly...to be sure, a fine upstanding bag of nuts as ever there was. His was the only other canoe we saw on the entire trip, and if there were ever two canoes that were at opposite ends of the spectrum, it was ours. From a distance it was difficult to make out exactly what kind of craft it was, what with it's yellow, black, and red camouflage paint job. Upon closer inspection, it was a miracle the thing even stayed above the waves. The aluminum gunwales ran every which way but straight and a heavy weave fiberglass cloth full of patches dotted the inside. Filling his boat were three fishing rods, a large crab trap, and two coolers full of beer. "Domestic or import?" as he so put it. As passersby inquired on his destination, he would enthusiastically reply, "Mexico!" We enjoyed John Jolly for two days, swapping stories of our adventures. We compared stories of the Mississippi, which he had paddled three years earlier. He also gave a more recent account of his being surrounded and attacked by a band of rogue raccoons. "The leader jumped through my campfire and charged towards me, bearing it's teeth and spitting violently. I shot him from about three feet. He rose up on his hind legs, clutched his chest, and dropped dead before me." We ended up losing John in the Ten Thousand Islands, but our meeting was a good distraction from the mundaneity of the Condo Coast.

Later that evening, a raccoon came into our campsite, stealing all of our fresh supplies and making off with Nile's only pair of pants! Go figure.

Feb. 21 – De Soto Park. The north wind blew hard all night and continues to do so all day, increasing to 25 mph in the afternoon. K.'s infection shows no signs of getting better, so I leave her on the beach and head out of the park in search of a drugstore. I walk 3 miles with my thumb out, but with no joy. Finally a park ranger pulls over to inform me that hitching is not permitted in the park. I explain the situation, but it's too much for him to comprehend. He flags down a cop car, and the three of us stand around discussing the situation. Vaginal infections, canoes, hitch hiking, and drug stores. Finally the police officer says he will give me a ride to the mainland, so there I am, sitting in the back of a cop car, getting a ride to the drug store. After getting the medicine, a bag of oranges, and some rolls, I start the long hot hike back to the park, about 10 miles. By about 4:30pm I get back to K., tired and blistered on both feet. We make camp deep into the mangroves since now the rangers know that we're on the island. For another night on Mullett Key, we go undiscovered.

Feb. 23 – Small island opposite Mullet Key. Had a wonderful and peaceful evening last night strolling on the beach and picking up all sorts of sea life and shells. Brought them all back to our picnic table and formed a collection. Found a ratty ole boat that had washed up. Woke up this morning with the wind still blowing strong out of the east. We decide to paddle around the east side of Mullet to Tampa Bay to see how bad it is. We're getting ants in our pants and are tired of waiting.

Feb. 24 – Start the morning with an in-depth conversation about the youth of America with Thor, a Norwegian science teacher. We have a leisurely paddle along the beaches of Anna Maria and Long Boat watching the now crowded shoreline pass to our left. The wind is still from the east and the gulf is calm. We camp on Lido Beach, but it's risky and many people walk by.

Feb. 26 - Nakomis. Nigel's Aunt Sylvia and Uncle Mike have a very unique style of entertaining...good food, good wine, and lots of heated discussion. It's always a pleasure to be in their midst... tempers flair and laughter abounds. We're grateful to them for being a part of this trip, as they were with our previous trip a few years ago. Then we stopped in by sailboat, this time by canoe. They think we're not doing much in the way of progression!

Mar. 1 - Small island near Cayo Costa. It's a beautiful place to wake up, and we are witness to the wildlife waking up too. Charlotte Harbor is calm, and we paddle to North Captiva, and then out to the Gulf. But the wind picks up and just before Redfish Pass we portage back into the harbor. The beach of North Captiva is beautiful and devoid of human habitation. In the afternoon the wind is stronger from the west and we surf along the coast of Sanibel before pitching the tent near the causeway to the mainland.

Mar. 2 - We paddle out across to Fort Myers in calm seas, but by midday the wind is blowing strong from the west and waves are breaking over the sides. From Lover's Key we jump into a mangrove-lined back water that cuts through Bonita Springs, and brings us out at Wiggin's Pass. It's hot. About 80 degrees. Yippee!

Mar. 3 - We are chased off the beach by swarms of bugs - sand fleas and no-see-ums - before the sun is up. The dawn is calm and clear. By 8:30am we land on Vanderbilt Beach. It's empty save for joggers and snowbirds. Arrive back at the boat around midday to find it surrounded by sunbathers. We paddle off towards Naples in choppy conditions, arriving a couple of hours later. The west wind is blowing steadily harder and the sun is beating down. Meet up with a crazy guy by the name of John Jolly - a jolly chap indeed.

Chapter IX
Wilderness to the End

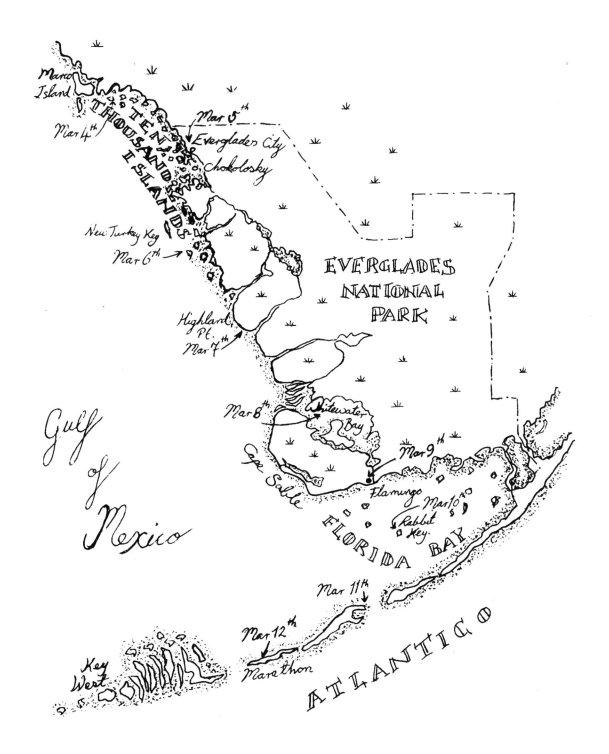

"I can safely say that I have no idea."
- Mark Baker

Chapter 9

Wilderness to the End

From Gordon Pass we hit the back waters all the way down to Marco Island. It was here that we purchased our first chart of the entire trip. We had been given a few old charts along the way, but for the most part we had navigated with road maps, tourist maps, or whatever free and not entirely useless information we could gather. But, for a place like the Ten Thousand Islands, a real chart is an extremely worthy investment. (That is unless you want to get lost, which has been the sole purpose of many that have come here...from the Seminole Indians to modern castaways, from Civil War runaways to Vietnam vets, from murderers to hermits. The folklore of the area is as rich as it's wildlife.)

The Ten Thousand Islands border the northwest corner of the Everglades National Park and it is exactly what it's name suggests. Ten thousand small mangrove islands, with great names such as Tiger Key, Panther Key, and Facahatchee, create a veritable maze of waterways. It is a popular fishing area and many of the locals make their living as fishing guides. It was in this area that we had a rather odd encounter with a vengeful manatee. The West Indian manatee is fighting a losing battle in it's coexistence with the human population of west Florida. Living in shallow coastal estuarine waterways, they are constantly hit by speeding boats and cut by their propellers. We have rarely, if ever, seen a manatee in these waters that does not display several propeller slash scars across it's back. Many manatees die from these terrible encounters. On this occasion it was the manatee's turn to give us a scare. Like a U-boat torpedo it headed for our midships, but at the last minute descended and skimmed underneath, leaving us shocked and rocking in the swirling water. "Let's get outta here!" Nigel shouted, and we paddled hard for Indian Pass and Everglades City.

Our long strange canoe trip had entered it's final stage. Nowhere is there a better place to end such a trip than with the beauty and abundant wildlife of the great everglades. Our first port of call was Everglade City, for if you wish to pass through the wildlife refuge, you are required to obtain a back country permit. This permit is astoundingly reasonable - for ten dollars a pop your party is allowed two weeks in the Everglades National Park, with campsites included. All camping arrangements must be cleared with the ranger when you purchase your pass, to ensure organization and safety, and to prevent over-crowding. In our case, the park warden seemed a bit shocked when we had no idea of the need for prearranged itineraries and spontaneously threw a four day itinerary together in five minutes. Four days was more time than we needed to pass through the Everglades, or to run down the coast, but we knew that in a week's time our adventure would be over. All too soon we would be back in the Keys, slogging it out at some dumpy Keys restaurant for minimum wage - so, of course we wanted to stretch out and savor these last few days. We walked into the town of Everglades City, which is more of a settlement than a town, for one last restocking of supplies, and then paddled down to the adjacent settlement of Chokoloskee to make camp.

One wonderful aspect of paddling and camping in the Everglades National Park is the variety of natural settings to chose from. There are over 40 campsites between Everglades City and Flamingo - of which 15 are coastal, 15 are inland platforms or 'Chikees', and 3 are islands in Florida Bay. There are two main routes through the park. The Wilderness Waterway is a marked trail that meanders for approximately 100 miles through the Glades' many rivers and lakes all the way to Flamingo on the north shore of Florida Bay. Alternatively, one can skirt the coastline, camping on beaches and small keys. We decided on the coastal route, mainly because we had no detailed maps of the interior and we had been into the Glades several times before.

Like every natural aspect of Florida, the Glades are under serious threat. The human population of south Florida continues to grow and the subdivisions of the Miami area continue to bite into a unique and fragile ecosystem. Once upon a time, water flowed freely from Lake Okeechobee south to Florida Bay, 'a river of grass' 120 miles long, 50 miles wide, and less than a foot deep. Thousands of birds flock here on their annual

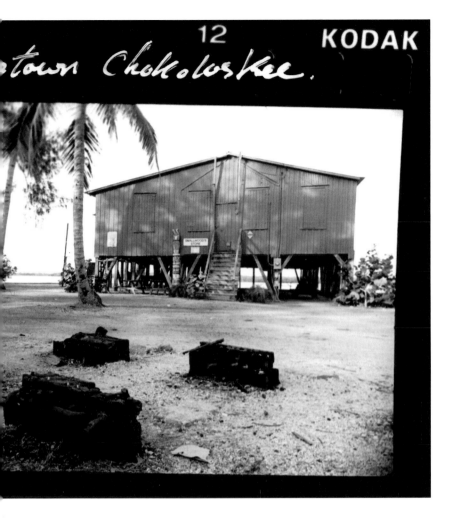

southern migration. There was a time not too long ago when the skies turned black from these flocks. It is a landscape where a few inches means the difference between high and low ground; a land dramatically defined by it's natural cycles of drought and flood, fire and sunshine; and a land that is the last habitat for endangered species such as the American Crocodile, Florida Panther, West Indian Manatee, Loggerhead Turtle, and Wood Stork. Today, canals, levees, and roads block and divert the water for ever-growing human use and much of the water that flows back into the Glades is contaminated by agricultural runoff, poisoning fish and birds, and making the gators sterile. We are walking on rice paper with oversized hiking boots. The Everglades and the wildlife that resides there are very much under threat of extinction. Unfortunately, with south Florida's building boom, it's insatiable appetite for money, and some people's need to live in a 'swamp' without bugs, we have created a monster that will only be satisfied when it has devoured everything including itself. But Mother Nature is a great adapter and we must live in hope.

The next four days were short paddling days. Usually by lunchtime we had reached our designated campsite, and spent the afternoons swimming, reading, beachcombing, and reflecting. The coastline is rugged, storm swept, and blissfully peaceful. Most of it is mangrove, but there are

March 4 - From Gordon Pass we hit back waters all the way down to Marco. We buy our first chart for the 10,000 Islands, head out and camp on Brush Island. Oh to have a real chart! We saw a distressed pelican with a hook in it's mouth, but we were unable to get close enough to grab and help him.

March 5 - Chokoloskee. We skirt along 10,000 Islands before cutting through Indian Key Pass to Everglade City. Another hot and beautiful day - 10 mph wind from NW. We get our back country permit and plan our route - $10 - a bargain for 5 nights of camping. A last trip to Everglade City for water and food, then paddle to Chok and stay at campground as guests of Katie and Ron from Indiana.

March 6 - A fine breakfast send off and into the Glades we go. Light wind, calm waters - hot and sunny. A perfect day. Finding our own path, we cut thru the maze of islands, just looking for open water. We paddle to New Turkey Key and camp by about 1 pm - a short day.

March 7 - Highland Point. A sandy stretch of coastline being invaded by thousands of horseshoe crabs laying their eggs in the sand. Another short day - hot and sunny. Slight east wind 10 mph. Oh, to be back in the real Florida, with no buildings in sight. No restaurants, no shops, no full service, no shoes, no shirt required. It's a prehistoric land, isolated and surrounded by the modern world.

March 10 - We're out here in the middle of Florida Bay on a tiny little piece of land, completely surrounded by water. Off of the horizon to the north is the mainland, from where we came so long ago, and off the horizon to the south is the end of our journey. Two more days. Just two more days...unbelievable. That's all we can say...unbelievable.

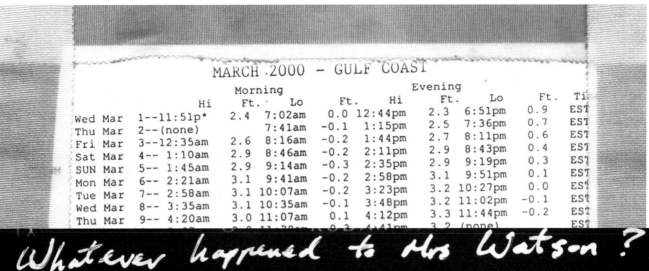

MARCH 2000 - GULF COAST

		Morning				Evening				
		Hi	Ft.	Lo	Ft.	Hi	Ft.	Lo	Ft.	Ti
Wed Mar	1--11:51p*		2.4	7:02am	0.0	12:44pm	2.3	6:51pm	0.9	EST
Thu Mar	2--(none)			7:41am	-0.1	1:15pm	2.5	7:36pm	0.7	EST
Fri Mar	3--12:35am		2.6	8:16am	-0.2	1:44pm	2.7	8:11pm	0.6	EST
Sat Mar	4-- 1:10am		2.9	8:46am	-0.2	2:11pm	2.9	8:43pm	0.4	EST
SUN Mar	5-- 1:45am		2.9	9:14am	-0.3	2:35pm	2.9	9:19pm	0.3	EST
Mon Mar	6-- 2:21am		3.1	9:41am	-0.2	2:58pm	3.1	9:51pm	0.1	EST
Tue Mar	7-- 2:58am		3.1	10:07am	-0.2	3:23pm	3.2	10:27pm	0.0	EST
Wed Mar	8-- 3:35am		3.1	10:35am	-0.1	3:48pm	3.2	11:02pm	-0.1	EST
Thu Mar	9-- 4:20am		3.0	11:07am	0.1	4:12pm	3.3	11:44pm	-0.2	EST

Whatever happened to Mrs Watson?

March 12- Florida Keys, Pull out of Fiesta Key early. Paddle gulfside past Long Key and Conch Key, now surveying the land for a piece of rentable real estate for ourselves, since after today we will be homeless. We pass under the arches of the old Flagler railway and over to the oceanside. It's a glorious day in paradise! In a few hours we come upon the sandbar where we had been married two years earlier. Although it is covered with the tide, we break for lunch and have a swim in the shallows. Another cycle has been completed. We give thanks to each other and to the Gods for letting us in, if just for a little while, on their mysterious plan. From here it's straight to Marathon, and to our favorite pub for some of Randy's "Fruity ass Shots"...and a whole lotta celebrating.

scattered beach areas, backed by dense growth of palms, strap ferns, slash pines, and strangler figs. Our eagerness to complete the trip faded completely away - we had no desire to give up this lifestyle which had exposed us to so much for so long. But it wasn't over yet.

The last obstacle to overcome was the 20 miles of open water in Florida Bay. Florida Bay separates the mainland and the Florida Keys. There are islands interspersed throughout the bay, yet all but three are completely overgrown and impenetrable. Our chosen course gave us only one island on which we could stop off to either rest or camp. All the other islands are brim full of mangroves with no shoreline to even step out on.

On the morning of March 10th we briefly listened to the radio, pulled out the compass, and set course for an island out beyond the horizon. Little Rabbit Key was it's name, strategically placed smack dab in the middle of Florida Bay. Everywhere you look there are little islands, little patches of green, but only one offered a safe refuge. In such circumstances, it is important to maintain a course, and we paused frequently to double check the compass, map, and ever-changing scene around us. We were looking for an island no bigger than a softball pitch. The mainland slowly dissolved behind us as mangrove islands materialized all around...between Frank Key and Catfish Key, past Pelican Key and Dildo Key, ..Dead Terrapin Key, Cluett Key, Rabbit Key, and finally, Little Rabbit Key. Thankfully Florida Bay turned out to be less of an obstacle and more of a final frontier to behold.

It was here that our trip really ended - and in no finer place could it have done so. As the afternoon rolled on, the clouds peeled back to reveal a big blue sky. The shallow multi-hued blues of Florida Bay shimmered under the tropical sun... and caught between it all, on an insignificant patch of green, we found ourselves exactly where we wanted to be. We swam all afternoon under the warm sunny skies, took a stroll through the meadow, and cooked an extravagant dinner. All that had occurred in the last five months would be reflected on later, but for now we just savored the moment, the solitude, and the beauty that our simple plan had brought us here. It was the first time in so very long that we truly had no concerns

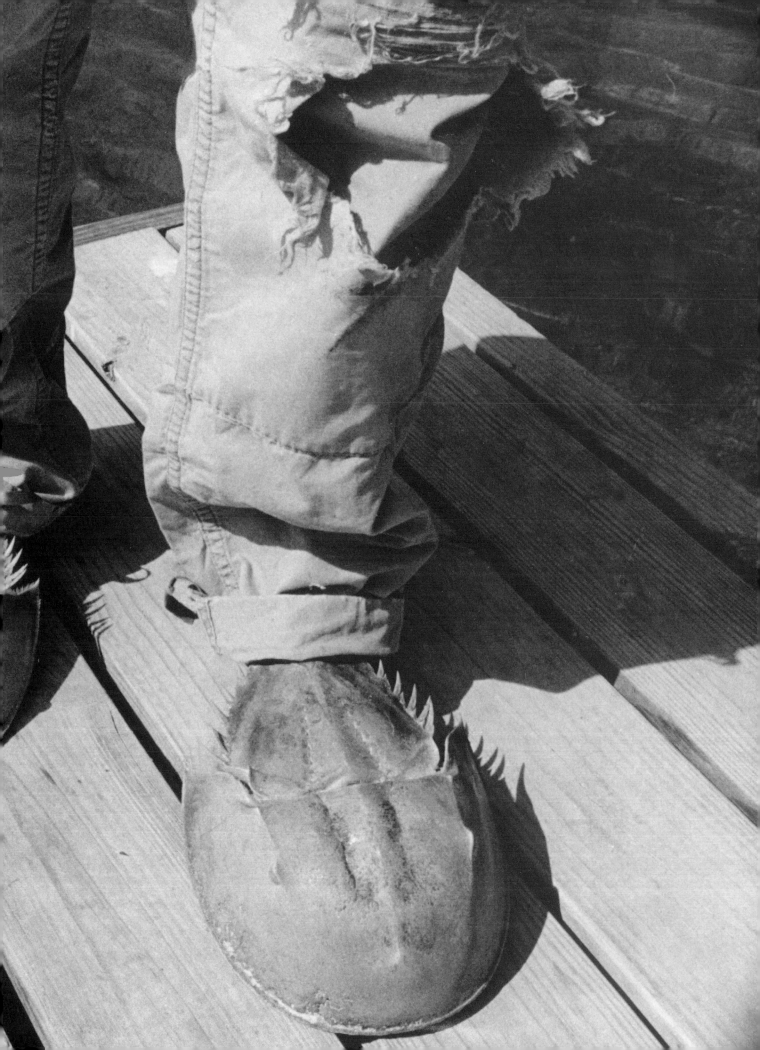

at hand. We knew that we had made it.

Well, we had almost made it. We pulled away from Rabbit Key the next morning under cloudy skies, with a brisk wind on our nose and squall clouds off to the west. The harder we paddled, the stronger the wind blew, until once again Kristin was going up and down like the Syrian Empire. The canoe rode over one wave and smacked down into the next. The Florida Keys were a distant blur and remained so for an agonizingly long time. For over three hours we paddled through gritted teeth with all of our might, locked in one last battle with wind and tide. Every other wave splashed over the bow and slapped Kristin in the face. If we didn't make landfall soon, we would be swamped and blown back from whence we came. Fiesta Key loomed on the horizon, but then ceased to loom and merely hovered. "Okay," said Nigel, "we're going to start paddling hard!" "What do you mean start??" shouted Kristin. The harder we paddled, the more we crashed through waves and the wetter Kristin got, so we backed off on the speed and just slogged it out. Ten miles and 31/2 hours later we landed on Fiesta Key - a KOA campground with a safe harbor and cozy little bar. Here the only interference from the weather outside came from the TV weather channel and an aerial map of the Keys covered in green snot. It wasn't too clear whether we were celebrating our arrival in the Keys, or just the fact that we were alive. At any rate, when we left the bar three hours later, we were rather surprised to find our canoe padlocked to the dock. After some discrete inquiries, we found out that we could only get the canoe released upon showing our camping permit. And so, with our boat chained like a criminal, we handed over our last few green backs, and apart from our permit in the Everglades, paid for our first real campsite since the start of the trip.

The paddle from Fiesta Key to Marathon was rather like driving down your home street after a long road trip...the postman gives you a friendly wave, unaware of your absence, and the neighbors peer out their curtains, noting your return..."They're back."

Chapter X
Epilogue

"It's a great day to ride."
- Brother Ray Crawford

Not The End

So, that's how we paddled to the Keys… smack dab through the middle of America and down it's inside right leg. It wasn't too difficult, but it wasn't easy either…in truth, we were almost as amazed as anyone else that we actually made it. Of course there were a few changes to our original itinerary - a couple of car portages and a ferry ride - but we were fine with that. It's not like we were out to prove anything. We simply wanted to get from Madison to Marathon and chose to do so by canoe. It took about 150 days longer than it would have by car, and cost us the better part of $2,000, but it gave to us memories that we will cherish for a lifetime and experiences that will be hard to beat. It was more than worth it. Granted, at times it was tough, and on a few occasions a bit scary, but the biggest obstacle that we had to overcome was doubting our own abilities. Given the chance, doubt will knock you out every time. As with all things, the fight comes from within, and success can only be achieved with persistence, hope, and a sense of humor. If you start a journey as we did with nothing else behind you, make sure you have at least these three things. Oh, and love.

We were extremely fortunate that the folks at Rutabaga and Wenonah believed in the merits of our plan. They made the trip possible with the kind loaning of some gear and our beloved boat. To them we will be forever indebted. Also, our parents have been wrung through the worry ladder not just a few times. They gave us their full support for this trip, as they have always done in the past with our hair-brained ideas. If they didn't support us, our lives would not be as rich as they are today. Thank you.

And so you ask, "And what of the Keys?" Well, you'll just have to go and see for yourselves. Or not.

The
FLORIDA
KEYS....

Bohemian Paradise...

.... or fractured fairy tale ?

Reporter: "So after paddling 2700 miles in a WeNoNah Champlain, how would you sum up it's handling characteristics?"

Kristin: "It's delicious!"

WE NO NAH

WeNoNah Canoes... Light, Fast, and "Delicious"!

PO Box 247, Winona, Minnesota 55987

(507) 454-5430

RUTABAGA

The Paddlesport Shop
220 West Broadway, Madison, Wisconsin 53716
1-800-I-PADDLE

"Not only do they carry the largest inventory of canoes and kayaks in the world, But they also hire some real professionals!"

Thank you and goodbye.